Poems From Central Southern Scotland

Edited by Angela Fairbrace

First published in Great Britain in 2008 by:
Young Writers
Remus House
Coltsfoot Drive
Peterborough
PE2 9JX
Telephone: 01733 890066
Website: www.youngwriters.co.uk

SB ISBN 978-1 84431 458 4

Foreword

Young Writers was established in 1991 and has been passionately devoted to the promotion of reading and writing in children and young adults ever since. The quest continues today. Young Writers remains as committed to the nurturing of poetic and literary talent as ever.

This year's Young Writers competition has proven as vibrant and dynamic as ever and we are delighted to present a showcase of the best poetry from across the UK and in some cases overseas. Each poem has been selected from a wealth of *Little Laureates* entries before ultimately being published in this, our sixteenth primary school poetry series.

Once again, we have been supremely impressed by the overall quality of the entries we have received. The imagination, energy and creativity which has gone into each young writer's entry made choosing the poems a challenging and often difficult but ultimately hugely rewarding task - the general high standard of the work submitted ensured this opportunity to bring their poetry to a larger appreciative audience.

We sincerely hope you are pleased with this final collection and that you will enjoy *Little Laureates Poems From Central Southern Scotland* for many years to come.

Contents

Newton Primary School, Dunblane

The Poems

Snowflakes

Snowflakes
Flying, spinning, tumbling,
Shining and magical,
Hides the mountains,
Cold and soft,
Snowflakes.

Calum McDonald

My Favourite Colour

Blue like the sky
Clear and shiny
Or the bright and wet sea.
Blue like school pencils
Dark and wooden
Or light rectangular word books.
Blue like dusty small chalk
Or heavy and hard snack baskets.

James Knott (8)
Colgrain Primary School, Helensburgh

My Favourite Colour

Green like peas, tiny, round and tasty,
Or apples, green, juicy and crunchy
Green like leaves in the summer
Or long grass
Green like frogs, slimy and wet
Or trees tall and long.

Rebecca Drysdale (8)
Colgrain Primary School, Helensburgh

My Favourite Colour

Blue, blue like the sky is blue, with bright clear clouds,
Or smooth nice-smelling bluebells,
Blue, blue the dolphins are blue, beautiful and gentle,
Or shells, shells, are blue, hard and different shades,
Blue, blue like the sea is blue, deep and wet,
Or a shark is blue, scary and frightening to
Everyone!

Chloe Williams (8)
Colgrain Primary School, Helensburgh

My Favourite Colour

White like lovely clouds in the sky,
Or paper for writing on
White like the board you write on
Or labels on dark things
White like chalk that you write with
Or a white top that you wear.

Emma Harrison (8)
Colgrain Primary School, Helensburgh

My Favourite Colour

Red like sweet, juicy strawberries
Or like a warm, cosy fire.
Red like yummy, crunchy apples,
Or like a spotty, beautiful ladybird.
Red like soft, lovely poppies,
Or like fabulous-smelling roses.

Jake Butler-Hoskin (8)
Colgrain Primary School, Helensburgh

My Favourite Colour

Red like the sunset, it is gorgeous.
The autumn leaves are red, crunchy and dry.
Red like the school top, bright.
Red, night is beginning and the clouds turn red.
Red like Spider-Man's suit because I like it a bit.
Some frogs are red, poisonous, big and slimy.

Anders Gillies (8)
Colgrain Primary School, Helensburgh

My Favourite Colour

White like puffy clouds,
Or doves that are so beautiful.
White like some soft fluffy snow
Or white paper that I can draw on.
White like snowflakes that are symmetrical,
Or a whiteboard that the teacher uses to write on.

Daniel York (8)
Colgrain Primary School, Helensburgh

My Favourite Colour

Red like rubies shiny and precious,
Or red like strawberries sweet and delicious.
Red like raspberries tasty as can be,
Or red like fire engines noisy and fast.
Red like Arsenal's strip, cool and smart.

Cameron Bolton (8)
Colgrain Primary School, Helensburgh

My Favourite Colour

Blue like the wonderful fantastic sky
Or like the wet, wavy sea.
Blue like a smooth, heavy dolphin
Or a beautiful, shiny sapphire.
Blue like soft, delicate raindrops
Or a tall, sharp wizard's hat.

Ryan Brown (7)
Colgrain Primary School, Helensburgh

My Favourite Colour

White like polar bears, sly and vicious
Or slippery, hard ice.
White like a pillow, soft and comfy
Or shiny, wet frost.
White like clouds, fluffy and beautiful
Or a hard, bumpy golf ball.

Emily Friels (7)
Colgrain Primary School, Helensburgh

My Favourite Colour

Blue like a bright cloudless sky
Or like a deep, dark sea.
Blue like a fast noisy waterfall
Or like a big bouncy trampoline.
Blue like a soft, comfy slipper
Or like a neat and tidy workbook.

Thomas Strettle (8)
Colgrain Primary School, Helensburgh

My Favourite Colour

Red as a letterbox, shiny and smooth,
Or a ladybird, spotty and tiny.
Red as a shiny and juicy apple,
Or a ruby, rough and round.
Red as leaves, soft and wet,
Or a poppy beautiful and soft.

Shania Beaty (8)
Colgrain Primary School, Helensburgh

My Favourite Colour

Yellow like the sun, bright and shiny
Or daffodils round and tiny.
Yellow like sweet juicy lemons
Or corn squishy and nice.
Yellow sand soggy and soft.
Or stars glittery and pointy.

Sarah Kemp (8)
Colgrain Primary School, Helensburgh

My Favourite Colour

Green like soaking tall grass
Or a shiny crunchy apple.
Green like a round and juicy cucumber
Or a small flying greenfly.
Green as a slow caterpillar with lots of legs
Or a log or dark stem of a flower.

Callum Williamson (7)
Colgrain Primary School, Helensburgh

My Favourite Colour

Red as the delicate rose petals
And as beautiful as you and me,
Or as cute and furry as the red panda
Who all day climbs in trees.
Red and rosy crunchy apples, stick to a tree with glee,
Or sweet and juicy as a cranberry
On a really hot day.
Red and colourful as a poppy
Which is gorgeous in the summer breeze,
Or would you prefer Santa's coat
Which is huge and cosy all round?

Niamh Macphail (8)
Colgrain Primary School, Helensburgh

My Favourite Colour

Red like the lovely, spotty, tiny ladybird
Or like shiny juicy apples.
Red like the dangerous hot fire
Or like the tasty strawberry.
Red like sweet raspberries
Or like a shiny, fragile ruby.

Niall Hogan (7)
Colgrain Primary School, Helensburgh

My Favourite Colour

Yellow like the burning hot sun
Or the beautiful clover that shines when it is wet.
Yellow like the smooth sand that scatters in the breeze
Or the stars that twinkle in the sky.
Yellow like the rough pollen that bees take
Or the glamorous topaz.

Rebecca Friels (7)
Colgrain Primary School, Helensburgh

My Favourite Colour

Blue like the lovely wonderful, blue shining sky,
Or the super lovely sea so blue.
Blue like a blue pen, so helpful and good,
Or my word log, incredible, which has amazing words.
Blue like beautiful blue-tac so nice
Or fire going *bang!* and flaming.

Ross Biagi (8)
Colgrain Primary School, Helensburgh

My Favourite Colour

Green like small wet grass,
Or a juicy apple.
Green like leaves on the top of the tree,
Or a big spotty frog.
Green like tiny peas,
Or a lollipop sweet and round.

Hassan Hussain (8)
Colgrain Primary School, Helensburgh

My Favourite Colour

Yellow like bananas, juicy and soft,
Or custard, hot and delicious.
Yellow like a melon, round and slippery,
Or sun burning and melting.
Yellow like lemon, sour and smooth,
Or sand grains tiny as a spot.

Fiona Porter (8)
Colgrain Primary School, Helensburgh

My Favourite Colour

Red like strawberries, juicy and sweet
Or like apples, crunchy and yummy to eat.
Red like ladybirds, tiny and spotty,
Or like fire, warm and cosy at home.
Red like your house, made out of red bricks,
Or red poppies, beautiful and they smell nice too.

Laura Bond (7)
Colgrain Primary School, Helensburgh

My Favourite Colour

Red is like a crunchy juicy apple
Or like slimy, watery blood.
Red is like a nice lovely ladybug
Or like tasty and sweet jam.
Red is like a red Remembrance poppy
Or like a nice sour strawberry.

Kirsty Rigby (8)
Colgrain Primary School, Helensburgh

3, 2, 1 . . . Blast Off!

The rocket goes whoosh
And flash
Shimmering with sweat
Dripping down your face.
The fire pushes it up,
It goes shooting into space,
Space has stars shining
Push a big red button.

Jack Veruschka (10)
Denbeath Primary School, Buckhaven

Five

Sweating, shaking
In my suit; buttons
Flickering on and off;
Sitting, waiting for
Instructions. *Four* . . . I
Press a button to put the
Heaters on; I start to sweat
Even more. *Three* . . . I feel
The sweat dripping off; the
Heaters get hotter and
Hotter. *Two* . . . Getting
Ready for take-off; people
Screaming, saying
Goodbye. *One* . . . the tower
Detaches; I feel too
Nervous to fly into space . . .
Lift Off.

Jordan Byers (9)
Denbeath Primary School, Buckhaven

Earth Scene

Float in a shuttle with no gravity
Holding you down.
Amazing, no ecstatic, it's Earth
Astronauts float with the stars,
Buttons and switches everywhere.
Food mixed with water makes
The perfect meal.
Cameras scan, nothing but
Space and darkness.

Bryony Millar (9)
Denbeath Primary School, Buckhaven

Bryony Millar
4/4/2008

In Space

I went up in a *whoosh!*
Sweating, nervously
Planets, Earth, stars,
Spinning in space
Flipping up and down.
I see Mars but I'm
Heading for the stars
Wow, butterflies in my tummy,
Spice food is yummy
Many miles from home
I'm just sitting here alone.

Shannon Mackie (10)
Denbeath Primary School, Buckhaven

Let's Go!

Sweating nervously in your seat
Hear people screaming
5, 4, 3, 2 1 ready to go
While the spacemen meet
The rocket will flow
Let's go, let's go to the stars
There are some sparks
Maybe we can see Mars
5, 4, 3, 2, 1 let's go to the moon
Bang! The boosters are lit up.

Rebecca Whitley (10)
Denbeath Primary School, Buckhaven

My Dog

My dog
Is as small as a puppy
Black with white splodges
Brown eyes staring up at me
Soft, furry coat to stroke.

My dog
Chases wildly around the garden
Jumps in the air for a ball
Wags her tail excitedly
Lies by her basket quietly.

Elle Wyatt (7)
Guildtown Primary School, Guildtown

The Car

A gleaming piece of machinery
It grips the road on every corner
Accelerates with lots of horsepower
Black tyres spinning along the road
Headlamps shining in the dark
Wipers waving on the window
Brown leather seats as smooth as ice.

Connor Key (10)
Guildtown Primary School, Guildtown

Dolphins

Dolphins dancing in the waves
Rushing through the ocean sea
Slimy as seaweed in the water
Having fun jumping up and down
Friendly and curious to find out what's happening
Chasing each other under the water.

Meaghan Wilson (10)
Guildtown Primary School, Guildtown

One Tiny Monster

One tiny monster sitting in a shoe,
Along came another one and that made two.

Two tiny monsters sitting in a tree,
Along came another one and that made three.

Three tiny monsters lying on the floor,
Along came another one and that made four.

Four tiny monsters hiding in a hive,
Along came another one and that made five.

Five tiny monsters having a Twix,
Along came another one and that made six.

Six tiny monsters flying up to Heaven
Along came another one and that made seven.

Seven tiny monsters giving fish some bait,
Along came another one and that made eight.

Eight tiny monsters, planting a vine,
Along came another one and that made nine.

Nine tiny monsters getting chased by a hen,
Along came another one and that made ten.

Jack Patterson (6)
Kettins Primary School, Blairgowrie

Tiger, Tiger

Tiger, tiger, orange golden fur like the sun.
In the sunset you will see her leap from branch to branch.
Her little cubs are as sweet as little kittens waiting for food.
But their mum has paws as big as a man's hand.
She walks straight like a king in a procession.

Matt Brown (10)
Kettins Primary School, Blairgowrie

Tiger

Tiger, tiger, you've daggers for eyes
You've chainsaws for claws
And a heart that's cold.

Tiger, tiger, you've a brain that's fierce,
You have legs to run,
You're just like us but so different.

Tiger, tiger, you look like Satan
But all you are is a *big cat!*

Niran Lewis (8)
Kettins Primary School, Blairgowrie

Tiger

Tigers are so beautiful,
Their stripes shine,
They sparkle like the sun.

You never know where they are,
They leap out like a spring,
But I think I love them!

Calvin Mustard (7)
Kettins Primary School, Blairgowrie

Tiger, Tiger

Tiger, tiger likes to eat. He's looking for a big, juicy treat.
He prowls with his claws? Sheathed out of his paws.
His eyes are bright? As shiny as a light.
He likes to fight, in the middle of the night.

Shaun Strachan (11)
Kettins Primary School, Blairgowrie

When The Snow Falls

When the snow falls
We like to have snowball fights.

When the snow falls
We can make igloos.

When the snow falls
We can make cakes.

When the snow falls
I wear a jumper and trousers.

When the snow falls
I cover myself in snow.

When the snow falls
I go sledging.

Chanice Mustard (6)
Kettins Primary School, Blairgowrie

My Tiger Friend

Here she comes, my tiger friend,
Slowly crawling through the grass,
Her eyes set on an abandoned deer
Thy life is coming to an end.

Look at me now,
See where I am,
Here I see my tiger friend.

I see the eye of thy cub,
As beautiful as you,
If he is like his mother, he is like thee.

Shannon Middleton (10)
Kettins Primary School, Blairgowrie

When The Snow Falls

When the snow falls
You can go sledging.

When the snow falls
You can have a snowball fight.

When the snow falls
You can go skating.

When the snow falls
You can make a snowman.

When the snow falls
You can hide.

When the snow falls
I dive in.

When the snow falls
It is very cold.

When the snow falls
I wear a hat, scarf and a jacket.

Jack McLean (7)
Kettins Primary School, Blairgowrie

Fearsome Stripes

Tiger, tiger in the jungle,
When I see her it makes me rumble.

Black and orange stripes on her body,
When she bleeds I feel so sorry.

Piercing eyes, terrifying paws,
Beautiful but terrifying claws.

Kerry Warden (9)
Kettins Primary School, Blairgowrie

The Space War

Cowboys with their leather belts
Always eating chocolate that melts.

Aliens with their bubble guns,
Always eating jelly buns,
Aliens hunting on the moon
While getting chased by a space baboon
Cowboys shooting ugly ducks
But they're scared 'cause they don't have the guts
Aliens flying to space
Even though they're a big disgrace
Cowboys on their way to space
Trying to solve the alien case
Bang! Bang! Bang! The aliens shoot
Zap! Zap! Zap! The aliens toot
Ah well who cares now?
They've all disappeared, so now we must bow!

Josh Miller (11)
Lady Alice Primary School, Greenock

Hobbies

Football, football, football
Most of my friends like football
Some of my friends don't
I watch football on telly
Some players are tall and some are small.

Wrestling is fun to watch, and fun to play
Something to do on a rainy day
I also play wrestling on a trampoline
I'm just like a jumping bean.

John Wilson (11)
Lady Alice Primary School, Greenock

Land Of Sweets

Land of sweets
I walked round the corner,
Chocolate button and candyfloss ceilings.
Candy pebbles on the ground
I eat marshmallows off the wall
Catching the chocolate football
As I stuff my face with After Eight Munchies.
When there is a fire
It makes Smarties melt inside
A chocolate mousse fire extinguisher
To cover the Smarties in sweet goodness
To make you eat it.
Maybe I should save it, or maybe not!
Yum-yum!

Ross MacDonald (10)
Lady Alice Primary School, Greenock

Summer Holiday

S ummer is the *best*
U mbrellas, I don't think so, at least I hope not
M y mum adores it
M y family loves and enjoys it
E veryone should like it
R ain I hope you don't come, you're not welcome.

H olidays are the best, no school, yippee!
O hh! Deckchair, I get to enjoy you
L ong lies in
I n the garden, out in the street, I still enjoy myself.
D ays without school
A hh days like this I really enjoy
Y es and I hope you enjoy it too.

Kimberley McFarland (10)
Lady Alice Primary School, Greenock

Wee Marc Atkins

Dear Marc,
Your name is often mentioned,
My thoughts are with you still,
You're gone but not forgotten,
What's more you never will.

Words are very few,
Thoughts are so deep,
Memories of you,
I'll always keep.

The emotions of people who knew you,
Were just so unbelievably true.

But we'll all meet one day,
Where everyone has to go,
You'll be glad to see me,
I'll tell you everything I know.

If you have any replies or questions,
Just send a wee kiss and a hug,
To the address above,
I'm sure I'll catch it through luck.

Get to work on that letter,
I mean it you'd better.

Kirsten McAteer (11)
Lady Alice Primary School, Greenock

Birds

The thing I like about life,
Is birds.
The way they float in the air,
Birds.

My favourite is the jay,
With their bright colours.
And the way they are so small,
Jay.

I also like the robin,
With their redbreast,
They way they come out at
Christmas,
Robin.

I love the graceful swan,
With their white feathers,
They glide along water,
Swan.

So these are the birds I like best,
There are so many,
I hope you like them too,
Birds.

Heather Ross (10)
Lady Alice Primary School, Greenock

Why Racism?

Racism, racism
Why always racism?
There is nothing wrong with being
A different colour
Why never purple?
Why never green?
We all play for the same team
Why never yellow?
Why never pink?
It is time people began to think.

Racism, racism
Stop this carry on
We're running out of time
Stop being so blind
Get together and talk
Before the clock stops.

Gemma Docherty (11)
Lady Alice Primary School, Greenock

My Best Friend

My best friend is Lucy
She is very funny.

We never fall out or go
In tantrums with
Each other.

My best friend is so
Hard-working, she
Never stops thinking of
Others.

My best friend is Lucy
And nothing will change
That.

Hayley McLaughlan (11)
Lady Alice Primary School, Greenock

The Alien Invasion

The aliens are coming,
We don't know what to do,
We're running on the streets,
They're coming after us,
They're catching us in cages,
Shooting us with lasers too,
The aliens are coming,
We don't know what to do.

The invasion has begun,
We're in need of desperate help,
One by one we disappear,
Being carried to the stars,
What's the point in fighting back,
The more we fight the hungrier they get,
The invasion has begun,
We're in need of desperate help.

Ben O'Hara (10)
Lady Alice Primary School, Greenock

Roller Coasters

Up and down and round and round,
Screaming there and then,
When I go on a roller coaster,
I never want it to end.

I feel as if I'm as high as the sky
When I'm at the top,
But next comes the dreaded drop,
Down and down and down we go.

Flying through the air,
I'm screaming as if I am losing my hair,
My eyes are starting to water,
As we come to a halt.

Oh what fun we have had today,
On this roller coaster.

Megan Adams (11)
Madderty Primary School, Crieff

My Dog Zac

My dog Zac is the greatest dog in the world,
He is strong and proud,
Even prouder than the proudest dad!
He loves his food and would never leave his bowl empty!
He is as warm as the sun and can run as fast as a cheetah.
He is the best in the world, even better than gold.
He is as strong as a heavyweight,
But my love for him is much stronger.

James Duguid (9)
Madderty Primary School, Crieff

The Skeleton King

It's Hallowe'en and the full moon is high.
The skeleton king comes riding by,
His cloak is flapping.

He is riding to the castle on the hill
Full of ghosts and ghouls to kill.
He rides up to the door knocking,
The skeleton king says, 'Can I come in?'

Freddie Dyer (11)
Madderty Primary School, Crieff

A Firework's Life

Silent at first,
But then a big burst of silver and green light,
It zooms overhead like a comet in space,
Then drops down like a dead fly,
Suddenly a strange sound, a whirling light,
Faster and faster,
Brighter and brighter,
Then *bang!* It's gone.

Noah Moray-Parker (8)
Madderty Primary School, Crieff

Rock Climbing

See jagged rocks
Hear the wild winds twisting
Taste soggy moss
Touch cold, hard rock
Crackling, crumbling rock falling down
I am scared
Hear the rope stretching
Slip
I am hanging
I am hanging in the air
I feel that I am flying when I am hanging
I land back on the rock
I start to climb
It gets colder as I go up and up
So I climb faster to keep warm
Near the top now,
I am almost there.

Haydn Donald (10)
Madderty Primary School, Crieff

Go-Karting

G ood fun
O vertaking people

K arting is the biz
A big adrenaline rush
R acing is very hard
T rying hard
I nteresting
N ever lost a race
G reat reliability.

Elliot Paterson (9)
Madderty Primary School, Crieff

Leaves

First a bud, all alone.
Then slowly the bud turns into a leaf.
Slowly another leaf appears.
Then all the buds slowly but surely turn into leaves.
They have woken to a lovely warm day in summer.
From the cold winter days they have been waiting until this day.
After a long time, autumn approaches
And the leaves start to fall and flutter.
Then the children come out to play.
They kick the leaves about.
Rustle, crunch, swish go the leaves.
Then it happens all over again . . .

George Ewing (8)
Madderty Primary School, Crieff

The Lightning Horse

There in the silent dark night I heard
Thunderous galloping.

At last I saw it! A black and white stallion.
It was tall with a big head,
A thick tail and a slim body.

I blinked and opened my eyes but it was gone.
It had vanished in a flash, as quick as lightning.

Fraser MacKenzie Simpson (9)
Madderty Primary School, Crieff

Colours

Colours, colours they are all around you.
Colours, colours like red and blue.
Colours, colours, green and yellow.
Colours, colours, they're great my dear fellow.

Conrad Downie (9)
Mill of Mains Primary School, Dundee

Haunted House

H aunted houses
A nd little bugs
L ots of ghosts
L oads of frights
O wls of the night
W hen midnight hits
E veryone runs
E very monster chases
N ever do the people come back.

Elise Teviotdale (9)
Mill of Mains Primary School, Dundee

The Christmas Day

It was Christmas Eve, I was very happy,
I couldn't wait for all the presents,
I was very sleepy but couldn't sleep.
I was too excited but I didn't hear a peep.
Santa will soon be here,
Close my eyes, hold them tight,
Let the moon shine bright
I hear the door . . . night-night!

Josh Skelly (10)
Mill of Mains Primary School, Dundee

Bonfire Night!

On Bonfire Night it's cold and exciting,
I love all the colours, bright and frightening.
I hear a rumble in my tummy,
My mum and dad think it's so funny.
I go back home and give a moan.
I curl up in bed and get my big ted.

Night-night!

Rebecca Laxy (9)
Mill of Mains Primary School, Dundee

Hallowe'en Horrors

My mother is a witch.
My father is a goblin.
My auntie is a werewolf.
My uncle is a ghoul.
My brother is a bat.
My sister is a vampire.
My cousin is a dragon.
My friend Bob is a killer bee.
I am the scariest of all
I am me!

Rachel Scott (10)
Mill of Mains Primary School, Dundee

Football Crazy

F antastic football is very good
O n the pitch I'm scoring goals
O h my I am the best
T eamwork helps you score
B alls are very hard
A ll the players have a good time
L ovely skills on the pitch
L ong time on the ball.

Andrew Scott (9)
Mill of Mains Primary School, Dundee

The Christmas Robin

Red robin, red robin, flying around my window.
Squeaking at Christmas time.
It's family time, red robin, red robin,
You should be with your family.
Goodbye red robin, it's Christmas time,
Red robin, red robin have fun!

Sholah Aitken (9)
Mill of Mains Primary School, Dundee

I Am An Evacuee

I hear the conductor shouting, 'All aboard!'
Striking fear into everyone
I see mothers weeping as children
Board the trains
I think about my foster family,
Will they beat me or will they like me?
I wonder if the war goes on long enough
Will I have to fight in this horrifying war?
I wish this war would end
So I could stay at home
I feel tense as my brother boards the train
Going to an unknown place
I am an evacuee.

Robbie Urquhart (11)
Newton Primary School, Dunblane

I Am An Evacuee

I am an evacuee standing in the rain
I feel discombobulated and alone getting on this train
I can see babies whining in the thick black smoke,
I can hear the whistle of the man on the train
And a constant buzz running through my head.
I hope I get a lovely homeowner
And have a good time
I have a slight fear of an air raid or getting killed.

I wish the war will halt soon,
And I'll be back in the city.

I am an evacuee.

Rory Thomson (10)
Newton Primary School, Dunblane

I Am An Evacuee

I am an evacuee
I see weeping children and parents crying
And praying that their children will be safe,
I hear the train coming into the station
And the thunderous planes from above.
I'm only small and very scared,
I fear my parents will get bombed in this frightening experience,
I wonder where my sister is, what if I get lost?
I want the Germans to stop bombing, I want this war to end now,
I hope the country people are friendly and caring,
I'm very anxious and nervous, but on the bright side,
Maybe it will be quite adventurous,
The train is here, I have to go,
I am an evacuee.

Emily Howitt (11)
Newton Primary School, Dunblane

I Am An Evacuee

I feel the ground shaking when the bombs fall
See from my window the sky lightning up
I fear that we will be the next victims of these horrible crimes,
I want the safety of my country
On the way to the station I see devastation
I see fallen houses and mangled cars
I hear the long scary sirens rushing around.

I feel worried about my parents.
I am not sure if I will be able to cope without them.
In the station there is an atmosphere of sorrow
And loss as children leave their crying mothers
I turn to look at my mum but she is crying too much.

Isaac Thomas (11)
Newton Primary School, Dunblane

I Am An Evacuee

I see a little girl drop her doll
And I think how sad she must be.
I feel like punching Hitler in the face
And ripping his stupid moustache off,
While bringing war to an end.
I want to bring my family with me so they will be safe,
And will not get hurt.
I think my heart could cut out any second,
My guts are squiggly
I think the Germans will bomb me.
I wonder if I will ever be reunited with my family and friends!
I hope Hitler will die and all the people who follow him.
I am an evacuee.

Keith Wright (11)
Newton Primary School, Dunblane

I Am An Evacuee

I feel worry spread through me from head to toe,
As I stand on the busy platform with people buzzing around me.

I hear children howling and mothers wailing,
As the train comes into the dismal station.

I wish that this war had not started,
As little children run around me, lost.

I see tears streaming down mothers' faces,
As they look anxiously for their children.

I hope everything will be happy again
And that I will be back here soon.

I am an evacuee.

Orla Stevens (10)
Newton Primary School, Dunblane

I Am An Evacuee

I am an evacuee

I feel the hot smoking air of the train on my face
And people pushing roughly past me.

I wonder who I'll be evacuated to
And hope they'll be kind to me.

I see shocked little children clutching their teddy bears
And teachers hustling us all together.

I hear train doors slamming shut
And mothers waving goodbye to their children.

I fear what people will think of me, a city child.

I worry about my family,
All alone in the city with bombs raining down on them.

I wish the war would end, so I cold rejoin my family.

Sarah Keen (11)
Newton Primary School, Dunblane

I Am An Evacuee

I wish this war would end and I could go to my loving family.
I see broken houses and wonder, *could that be my own?*
I feel desperate, I want to see my mother and father.
I hear squeaks of the train, and the cries of the children
wanting their parents.
I fear for my parents, are they going to be bombed?
Are they even alive?
I think to myself, *where am I going?*
What's happening?
I hope that dreadful Hitler loses his power and I can go home.
I am an evacuee.

Cameron Ross (10)
Newton Primary School, Dunblane

I Am An Evacuee

I am an evacuee,
I see the shapes of children standing quietly on the cold, damp
platform,
I hear the disturbing bustle of people on either side of me,
I feel my white hand shaking unstoppably,
I think about my mother, heartbroken, as I go off to safety; she is
stuck at home,
I hope desperately I'll make new friends in the radiant countryside,
I hope I will see every cheerful face I know again,
I think I will cry,
I feel my heart thumping loudly,
I hear the train's shrill whistle, it means I have to go,
I see the smoky train waiting for me,
I feel a hot tear staining my rosy cheek,
I am an evacuee.

Louise Mitchell (11)
Newton Primary School, Dunblane

I Am An Evacuee

I am an evacuee,
I feel the tension of everyone on the station platform,
I hear the eternal buzz of conversation as I stand fearful,
on the platform,
I wish someone would stop this madness and stop the evil that
started it,
I see the mixed emotions on people's faces, pondering on where
they're going,
I think of my brother and sister,
Wondering if they're unharmed,
I fear for their safety,
I hope I will have a kind family in the country.
I am an evacuee.

Neal Ramsay (11)
Newton Primary School, Dunblane

I Am An Evacuee

I feel my heart beating fast with anxiety as I stand, lost, at the station,
I see through the billowing smoke from the train, people
waving goodbye,
I hear people softly weeping as I get into the train,
I fear that the ones close to me might die,
I feel an air of sadness as the train chugs slowly along,
I wonder what will happen at the end of this long, miserable journey,
I hear people getting off at each stop and wonder when it will be
My turn,
I wonder if I will like my new life in the place that seems alien to me,
I want this unhappiness to end and for things to be normal again,
I hope this horrible, unforgettable war stops soon,
I am an evacuee.

Katy Smith (10)
Newton Primary School, Dunblane

I Am An Evacuee

I am an evacuee
I feel lonely, as if the world doesn't want me
I see mothers weeping and children looking bewildered as they
climb onto the train
I hope this horrible war will be over soon so we can return to our
families and friends
I hear loud buzzing sirens and yelling everywhere,
I feel lost, as if the world is over
I wish for my family, I wonder where my sister is
I hope my new house will be great, and my family will survive
the war,
I am an evacuee.

Eilidh Ironside (10)
Newton Primary School, Dunblane

I Am An Evacuee

I am an evacuee,
I hear the whistle blowing while another train goes by,
to the next unknown destination,
I fear the hated war will never end and the bombs may never
stop falling,
Wave after wave after wave.
I wonder how long all my family and friends will be able to live without their street being bombed,
I see a row of tenement flats destroyed by the devilish German
bombers.
I see the train pulling in at the station, the black smoke billowing out of the funnel, looming like the unknown home I know I will have
to face.
I hope the bad news, rationing and the dreaded bombs which cause so much despair will end,
I am an evacuee.

Cathal McIver (11)
Newton Primary School, Dunblane

I Am An Evacuee

I am an evacuee!
I see small confused children not letting go of their parents' woolly
warm coats,
I hear mothers and children weeping in dismay,
Not knowing if they will ever see each other again,
I feel small and bewildered as I stand petrified on the cold train
station platform,
I wonder if the detestable war will ever end,
How long will I be in the countryside for?
I want everything to end and for us all to be an idyllic family again,
I know I have to be brave, but I am so perplexed and just wish
Everything would be normal again.
I am an evacuee!

Caitlin Reid (11)
Newton Primary School, Dunblane

I Am An Evacuee

I hear people crying from the pain of leaving their families.
I feel petrified about the countryside.
I wonder what's going to happen to me.
I want my mum and dad back.
I hope that we'll all be together again.
I see mums with worried looks on their faces.
I fear that my mum might be bombed.
I am an evacuee.

Jack Matthewson (11)
Newton Primary School, Dunblane

I Am An Evacuee

I see lots of people sobbing and waving,
As I stand waiting for the train
I feel nervous for I fear the owners of the house will not like me,
I hope my parents are safe and my house has not been blown up,
I think of what the countryside looks like as I wait for the train.
I hear the whistle blowing as the train pulls into the station.
I am getting on the train.
Now I am an evacuee.

Joe Young (11)
Newton Primary School, Dunblane

I Am An Evacuee

I hear nervous, sad laughter and crying children,
I see mums running to say goodbye before they get on the train,
I hope my family will survive,
I fear I might get lost in this huge, scary train station,
I feel sick because I am so worried about going to the countryside,
I wish my dad was here to say goodbye to me, and not at war,
I think war should never have started,
I am an evacuee.

Sarah Huggett (11)
Newton Primary School, Dunblane

I Am An Evacuee

I see crying children as I walk to the train.
I hear the whistle blowing as the train starts to move,
I want to stay with my parents and the war to end.
I feel I will be alone for the rest of my life,
I wonder what is out there the whole world round,
I know I will be safer when I go to the countryside.
I hope I will not be parentless when I come back.
I am an evacuee.

Ryan Sweeney (10)
Newton Primary School, Dunblane

I Am An Evacuee

I see children weeping on the platform.
I hear the train booming through the tunnel,
I feel overcome by fear of bombs,
I smell acrid smoke from the ammunition factories
I wonder if I will ever come back to the city?
I want my family to come with me, so they don't suffer this
terrible ordeal.
I am an evacuee.

Ross Parker (11)
Newton Primary School, Dunblane

I Am An Evacuee

I see hundreds of children saying goodbye,
I fear my parents will die
I feel scared, something bad will happen,
I think, *what will I see?*
I wish this whole thing had never happened
I am an evacuee.

Lorne Rutherford (10)
Newton Primary School, Dunblane

Wallace Monument

W allace Monument has some lovely views
A nd statues
L ots and
L ots of people come to see William Wallace's real sword
A t the top you
C an see the River Forth and
E very house in Stirling.

M any
O f the floors are about the battle of Stirling Bridge
N ice souvenirs can be bought at the shop
U nder the first floor there is a dungeon
M onument is very high
E very floor has a
N ice display of
T ough wooden statues.

Jamie Murray (9)
Newton Primary School, Dunblane

Wallace Monument

W allace Monument is so high
A nd when you get to the top it's like you will fall
L ook out and you can see for miles and miles away
L ike you're on top of the world
A nd it can fit in the space of your hand
C an you see Stirling Bridge?
E xcellent views all around.

M uch to do
O n the inside of the Wallace Monument
N ever nothing to do
U ntil you've been all over the
M any floors inside you can stay the
E ntire day and
N ever get bored
T he Wallace Monument is the best!

Kathryn Wright (9)
Newton Primary School, Dunblane

Wallace Monument

W allace was a very fearless
A nd cunning man
L oved by the people but
L oathed by the English,
A nd he was nicknamed Long Shanks,
C ertainly the
E nglish were afraid of him.

M any people climb the steps to get
O n to the top of the monument
N owadays we let the English go
U p to the top
M any people climb and
E veryone enjoys the view
N o more wars
T he Scots are victorious.

Cameron McEwan (8)
Newton Primary School, Dunblane

Wallace Monument

W ow what a sight
A nd lots more to see
L ots to learn, come on
L ots to see
A t the very top, ahh
C ars are driving lower down
E veryone enjoying the view I think.

M onument up high, we climb for life
O n the top it is very high
N ever it will let you down, upon the view
U p, up, up we go
M onument is very high
E veryone has had fun
N ow we have to go from the
T op!

Emma Duncan (8)
Newton Primary School, Dunblane

I Am An Evacuee

I am an evacuee
I feel bewildered, as I stand on the buzzing platform
I fear the personality of the person I am going to be billeted to;
I hope they are kind.
I wonder if the atmosphere will be the same in the countryside
as it is the city?
I hear the conductor call us to the carriage of fear,
I feel my heart pounding against my ribs
I hope that I will make friends in my new home,
I wish I could take everyone I ever liked with me to the country.
I wonder if I will catch an illness in my new surroundings
I am an evacuee.

Greg Pascazio (11)
Newton Primary School, Dunblane

I Am A Scottish Soldier

I see people dying, mainly my friends,
I smell the marsh swish-sloshing under people's feet,
I taste blood from my sore cheek,
I hear the slish-slosh of horses galloping and sinking in the marsh,
I feel like I shouldn't be doing this,
I am a Scottish soldier.

Katie Gordon (8)
Newton Primary School, Dunblane

I Am A Scottish Soldier

I see the English charging on their horses
I smell the dirty water splashing in my face
I taste the blood from my cut
I hear the swords clashing together
I feel sad and angry in case we don't get peace
I am a Scottish soldier.

Stephanie Lilley (9)
Newton Primary School, Dunblane

I Am A Scottish Soldier

I am a Scottish soldier
I see enemies with dangerous weapons
I smell gas and lots of blood
I taste blood and the metallic taste of my helmet
I hear lots of screaming
And angry people
I feel scared and frightened
And very angry
I am a Scottish soldier.

Louis Mateu (9)
Newton Primary School, Dunblane

I Am A Scottish Soldier

I see the English and their horses coming,
I smell the horses, marsh and blood,
I taste the water splashing in my face,
I hear the death cries of others,
I feel nervous and cautious in case peace won't come
Once the civil war is over,
I am a Scottish soldier.

Tara Heneghan (9)
Newton Primary School, Dunblane

I Am A Scottish Soldier

I am a Scottish soldier
I see the men dying
I smell the blood of the men dying
I taste the blood and tears of the men
I feel the English dying from the blade of my sword
I hear crying of the men dying.
I am a Scottish soldier.

Ciaren Ross (9)
Newton Primary School, Dunblane

I Am A Scottish Soldier

I am a Scottish soldier
I see Wallace's shiltron covered in the blood of Englishmen
I smell the dead bodies from both sides
I taste the dead Englishman's blood, it is horrible
I hear horrible screams of the people dying
I feel fear and victory, I fear I will die and I feel victory
Because we are winning.
I am a Scottish soldier.

Sophie Dodds (9)
Newton Primary School, Dunblane

I Am A Scottish Soldier

I am a Scottish soldier,
I see the English charging on their giant horses,
I smell sweat from my own forehead from nerves,
I taste blood coming up from my throat
I hear screams and shouts from dying people
I feel determined to win because the English are invading our land
I am a Scottish soldier.

Sara Morrison (9)
Newton Primary School, Dunblane

I Am A Scottish Soldier

I see people fighting and about one minute later they die.
I smell the horrible smell of blood.
I taste horrible muddy water.
I hear swords clashing and men crying.
I feel really worried that I'll lose my life.
I am a Scottish soldier.

Victoria Prior (9)
Newton Primary School, Dunblane

I Am A Scottish Soldier

I am a Scottish soldier
I see the English enemies on the other side of Stirling Bridge.
I smell the marsh land and the bog
I taste blood from my wounds and cuts
I hear the sounds of screaming and shouting
And people falling into the river
I feel scared and uncertain thinking *should I be doing this?*
I am a Scottish soldier.

Rhona Stevens (9)
Newton Primary School, Dunblane

I Am A Scottish Soldier

I see the arrows of the English bowmen
I smell the blood of the horses that are running into the shiltron
I taste the blood running down off my chainmail and into my mouth
I hear the clashing of the English and Scottish swords
I feel the hand of the man next to me on my leg because he just got
hit by an arrow
I am a Scottish soldier.

Finn Thomas (9)
Newton Primary School, Dunblane

I Am A Scottish Soldier

I am a Scottish soldier
I see spearmen throwing their spears
I smell the muddy water splashing onto my helmet
I taste the metal of my helmet
I hear people screaming
I feel scared and weird
I am a Scottish soldier.

Stewart Wilson (9)
Newton Primary School, Dunblane

I'm A Scottish Soldier

The awful enemy are attacking
I see the massive horses in their battle robes.
They look powerful, scary and vicious,
Men in glinting armour shining in the sun.

I hear screaming men, squelchy mud,
Men falling into the river.
Creaky planks, the enemy horn, dying men,
Horses galloping into battle,
The enemy squires calling to their lords.

I taste blood and sick in my mouth
The sweat rolling down my face, the mud from the marsh
Being flicked up into my mouth.

I smell blood, horse dung, and mud, sweat,
Metallic armour and the odour of horses covered in sweat.

I feel sad, relieved that it's over,
I also feel angry, annoyed, one of my friends is dead,
It's terrible, I think I'm going to be sick.

Jurriaan Gouw (9)
Newton Primary School, Dunblane

I Am A Scottish Soldier

I see English charging towards me,
English men stomping into blood on the grass, their armour shining
in the sun.

I hear English men marching towards me, shouting 'Argh!'
Horses' hooves running along the ground.

I taste blood on the ground, wet armour everywhere.

I smell sweat and blood in the air, fear in the air.

I feel relieved that we've won the battle.

Emma Ferguson (9)
Newton Primary School, Dunblane

Wallace Monument

W illiam Wallace was a Scottish hero
A ll the nobles in Scotland liked him
L ives were being wasted with war
L onely children get diseases
A fter years they got freedom
C langing of swords
E levators they had none.

M onuments are very old so be careful
O nly one set of stairs
N o one doesn't enjoy climbing it
U nique patterns everywhere
M ore people visit it every year
E ven the English were scared of him
N obody wants it to fall down
T here was a monument made to remember him.

Natalie Young (9)
Newton Primary School, Dunblane

Wallace Monument

W ow you will say, because it is such an
A mazing sight
L ovely view of the
L ovely city
A mazing height and an amazing
C limb
E nergy is needed to climb.

M assive monument
O n a giant hill
N othing higher, all is
U nder
M ega climb 3 stops
E very stop full of fun
N ever want to go once at the
T op!

Max Pascazio (9)
Newton Primary School, Dunblane

I Am A Scottish Soldier

I see powerful, fearsome soldiers marching towards me,
Big metal shields with the soldiers' coat of arms,
Soldiers in their frightening, fancy metal armour,
The flag with all bright colours.

I hear the screams of death,
The horn blows, we all charge forward squelching underfoot,
The war cry of the English, the bridge creaks,
And then I can even hear the sound of my own heartbeat.

I taste the sweat dripping down my forehead and blood from
my nose,
Terrible taste of fear and hatred for the English.

I smell the scent of squelching mud under my feet,
And the blood of every being and rotting flesh.

I feel sad for my friend is dead and I fear I'm going to join him!

Catriona Lindsay (9)
Newton Primary School, Dunblane

I Am A Scottish Soldier

I see Andrew Murray and William Wallace leading the Scots.

I hear clashes of swords, cries of help,
Squelches of mud, splashes of water,
And the creaking and groaning of the bridge.

I taste horrible blood, sweat, tears and the fear and excitement
Of the Scots and the English.

I smell red blood, salty sweat, grass splattered with blood,
Thick, dark mud and brassy armour.

I feel a hand that had been cut off brushing past my head
And blood and sweat oozing out of my body.
I feel utterly exhausted and relieved it's all over.

Amy Morrison (9)
Newton Primary School, Dunblane

I Am A Scottish Soldier

I see the approaching army of doom,
The gruesome English king, King Edward I,
The bloodthirsty look on the English faces,
As they march towards us, arms raised.

I hear the sound of my heart beating like a drum,
Horses galloping to kill
The blood-curdling cries of my friends,
The impossible, my best friend, *dead!*

I taste my tears of sadness,
My friend's blood, as I try to bring him back,
The Englishman's fear as I kill him with triumph,
For I have avenged my friend,
I smell the sweet smell of grass that has been trampled on,
The smell of horse blood as they fall to their death.

I taste the blood coming from me, as I am ambushed by an
English soldier,
I feel that death is near, as the soldier tears me apart.

Anwen Davies (9)
Newton Primary School, Dunblane

I Am A Scottish Soldier

I see lots of blood, dead English soldiers,
Flying arrows, red grass, shiny chain mail,
Wet bodies, and a wooden bridge.

I hear shouting, screaming, splashing, metal clashing,
People marching across the bridge.

I taste acid in my mouth, blood running down my throat,
Mud in-between my teeth and I hate it.

I smell sweat, blood, metal smelly bodies,
Salty water, they are all horrible.

I feel wet, sore, tired, helpless, and happy that it is over at last.

Paul Kennedy (9)
Newton Primary School, Dunblane

I Am A Scottish Soldier

I see marching feet of the English coming towards us,
Some of the men on horseback, carrying heavy, shiny armour.

I hear bodies getting trampled on,
Swords and spears killing everyone in sight.

I taste the tears coming from my eyes as one of my friends has died.
Blood is coming from my face, I have had a small scratch.

I smell the grass getting stood on as the English charge into battle,
The mud is flying into my face from the people in front kicking it.

I feel the sun glowing on my face, but the terrifying feeling of not
Being able to see my family again, flows through my body.

Nathan Hendren (8)
Newton Primary School, Dunblane

I Am A Scottish Soldier

I see warriors ducking behind their shields
They are also making a shiltron.
I smell the blood of the great warriors who are injured.
I taste the horrible marsh going into my mouth.
I hear the clashing of swords hitting off the helmets.
I feel scared that I might die in the war like all of my brothers.
I am a Scottish soldier.

Rebecca Raw (9)
Newton Primary School, Dunblane

I Am A Scottish Soldier

I see shining new sharp swords ready to fight.
I hear the loud splash of soldiers falling in the water.
I taste strong wet blood and tears from my cheek.
I smell mushy, muddy, damp grass as we trample over it.
I feel relieved and tired, glad that the battle has ended.
We won! I am a soldier of Scotland who is still alive.

Marianne Donald (9)
Newton Primary School, Dunblane

I Am A Scottish Soldier

I see fierce Englishmen crossing the bridge,
Some on big strong horses charging with men covered in
heavy armour,
Swords clashing and big terrifying battle axes cutting people and
Wounding them, men falling into the river.

I hear men crying from painful wounds, men squelching in the very
deep mud,
People screaming when they get stabbed,
Men shouting when they fall in the water, the bridge creaking
and cracking.
Blood dripping down my face into my mouth, people in front
Kicking mud up into my mouth.

I taste grass flung up into my mouth,
The taste of water over my face from people splashing in the river.
I smell the grass that has been trampled by men,
I smell the metallic smell of blood from men.

I feel the pain of wounds on me, I feel sweat running down
my forehead,
And the sun gleaming against me.
I feel sick because I might not see my family again.

Niall Gilhooly (9)
Newton Primary School, Dunblane

I Am A Scottish Soldier

I see the English army marching towards us with big banners,
Huge war horses, with Englishmen on their backs,
Arrows flying through the air.

I hear screams, people dying, people shouting, horses galloping.

I taste blood, sweat pouring off people.

I smell metal, crushed grass and the swampy mud.

I feel excited, scared and nervous.

Ross Douglas (9)
Newton Primary School, Dunblane

I Am A Scottish Soldier

I see swords, axes and daggers all crashing, banging,
Fighting for victory,
Arrows flying through the air killing hundreds of people.

I hear people screaming and shouting,
Stabbing of the swords,
Clanging and banging of the swords and axes all fighting.

I taste tears coming out of my eyes and coming into my mouth,
And sweat trickling down my face.

I smell the grass that is covered in blood,
The chain mail and all the horses charging towards me.

I feel sweat trickling down my face and the blood that is coming
Down my arm and I felt beaten.

Bethan Evans (9)
Newton Primary School, Dunblane

I Am A Scottish Soldier

I see all the black and brown horses and the silver shiny swords.
All the English coming over the hill.

I hear people yelling and the English shouting
All the horses galloping, squelching on mud.

I taste sweat falling from my face.

I smell blood all over the place, and the trampled grass
And also the blood from the person I just stabbed.

I feel very happy that I won and very sad because my best friend
just died.

Emily Wright (9)
Newton Primary School, Dunblane

I Am A Scottish Soldier

I see well-equipped knights on horseback,
Glinting metal in the sunlight,
Vicious bowmen with arrows of death,
Bloodthirsty soldiers and William ready to signal our attack.
There are flags of many colours, swords ready to kill
And shields defending the evil.

I hear shouting men, galloping horses, squelching mud,
Clashing swords, whooshing arrows and cries of horror.
William blew the horn.
The battle had begun . . .

I taste my wounds, my blood and lots of fear.

I smell rusted metal, guts on the grass, flies as they have their feast.
Stinking mud is in the air but blood, I can smell everywhere.

I feel my sword hitting the enemy, the enemy's forces cutting
through ours,
And I feel the same pain as my dying friends.

James Gibson (8)
Newton Primary School, Dunblane

I Am A Scottish Soldier

I see bloodthirsty English, horses charging towards me,
Huge shields and swords getting closer and closer.

I hear squelching marsh and the sound of the bridge falling down,
Horses' hooves on the bridge, people are screaming and crying.

I taste blood and muck, water, grass, steel and acid.

I smell blood and marsh and steel and grass and horses and sweat.

I feel very scared and excited and worried.
I think I am going to be sick, but I feel happy it is over.

Craig Ivatt (8)
Newton Primary School, Dunblane

I Am A Scottish Soldier

I see crowds of men, their swords swishing and their axes falling,
There are men falling, clutching wounds and others swiping
and stabbing.

I hear petrifying bellows of fighting soldiers and the terrified screams
Of the wounded and the clashing of swords on armour.
I hear myself scream.

I taste fear beyond fear along with blood and sweat.

I smell the horrid smell of blood and sweat,
Animal dung and breath.

I feel horribly frightened and there is pain swarming over my body,
Along with pity for those who have to die.

David Hughes (9)
Newton Primary School, Dunblane

I Am A Scottish Soldier

I see bloodthirsty English charging towards me on huge war-horses
With steel armour gleaming in the morning light.

I hear Wallace's horn loudly echoing over and over,
Almost deafening me as I run towards the first English on sight.

I taste the blood from my lip and fear, and sweat.

I smell blood everywhere I go,
And thick brown oozing mud too.

I feel happy and relieved that it is over,
And I am still alive as I walk home.

Hannah Totten (9)
Newton Primary School, Dunblane

I Am A Scottish Soldier

I see bloodthirsty English soldiers charging towards us,
Claymores held up high, armour glinting in the sun.

I hear the cry of someone being killed, the squelch of the mud
Under my feet, the clip-clop of horses' hooves and steel to steel.

I taste blood that has been splattered on my face,
The sweat running down my face.

I smell a bloody smell and odour from the other soldiers.

I feel agonising pain because one of my hands has been chopped
Off by an English soldier.
I also feel scared because I could die.

Euan Lambert (9)
Newton Primary School, Dunblane

I Am A Scottish Soldier

I see people fighting with swords clashing together and people dying.
People falling in the water, people sliding in the mud,
People crying and sleeping.

I hear people dying, people screaming and I can hear people falling into the water,
People panting and groaning in the battle.

I taste blood in my mouth, and I can taste saliva in my mouth.

I smell the grass that has been trodden on.
I can smell the sword that had been in my hand.

I feel the sword in my hand, my hand has dry mud in my fist.

Sean Huggett (9)
Newton Primary School, Dunblane

I Am A Scottish Soldier

I see lots of angry-looking English soldiers marching towards us.

I hear swords clanging against each other.
I hate the sound,

I taste red blood coming into my dirty mouth.

I smell lots of horrible smelly sweat coming off faces and bodies.

I feel my wet dirty axe falling to the ground.

After all that war I was relieve, we won, but I had lost some of my best friends,

But I can't wait until I see my family.

Alison Fraser (8)
Newton Primary School, Dunblane

I Am A Scottish Soldier

I see English soldiers running and horses galloping really fast.
I hear knights shouting, 'England, England.'
I taste blood gushing into my mouth, and dripping down my head.
I smell smoke, logs burning, sweat on my hair,
Painful hands from holding my sword and running for miles.
I feel scared, upset because my friend is dead
And hurt because a spear pierced my foot.

Jake Wright (9)
Newton Primary School, Dunblane

I Am A Scottish Soldier

I see the English army in front of me looking fierce with anger.

I hear suddenly, the warning signal from Wallace up on the hill.

I taste fierce anger building throughout my body.

I smell blood from the English troops.

I feel scared that today could be my very last . . .

Molly Howitt (9)
Newton Primary School, Dunblane

Water

Huge geysers exploding,
Gentle harmless fog making cars slow down,
Evaporating steam rising into the air,
The same as when it comes out of a kettle,
Fluffy clouds moving gently through the sky,
Moving water vapour disappearing in the air,
Wet mist separating when cars drive through it.

In the sky the rain is pouring down from the clouds,
Lots of popping bubbles in the bath,
Swirling big black whirlpools in the sea,
Tall waterfalls splashing at the bottom of the stream,
Long lakes splashing against the rocks.

Beautiful snowflakes, shaped like a hexagon,
Falling from the sky,
Huge icy icebergs, boats crashing into them when they go past,
Solid slippy ice cubes melting in your hands,
Pelting hailstones falling from the sky,
Dropping snow, people throwing snowballs.

That's water!

Sophie Gilchrist (8)
Newton Primary School, Dunblane

I Am A Scottish Soldier

I see metal armour shining in the sun and lots of dead soldiers
lying on the grass.

I hear soldiers screaming in pain.

I taste fear and sweat dripping from my face and my hair.

I smell squelching mud and metal armour.

I feel pain, sick and very tired.

Nathan Batchelor (8)
Newton Primary School, Dunblane

Water

Water vapour, hot as the flaming sun
Floating high in the sky,
Turning into clouds in the sky,
Flying high,
Very black means rain or snow or hailstones.

Water makes waterfalls
Lakes, ponds, rivers, seas, lochs,
Floods, puddles and rain.

Ice, hard like rock,
Hailstones like pebbles,
Snow like ice, but softer.

That's water!

Stuart Elliott (7)
Newton Primary School, Dunblane

Water

Steam swirling,
Fog that is slow,
Fog that is fast,
Fluffy clouds floating,
Rising fog that is scary.

Wet and shiny, runny raindrops,
Falling from the sky,
Flowing, splashing water.

Ice that is slippery,
Cool and cold,
Melting slowly.

That's water!

Ethan Bennett (8)
Newton Primary School, Dunblane

Water

Geysers exploding,
Fog and mist down in the valleys,
Evaporating steam floating in the air,
Swirling and whirling,
Swishing, swashing, fluffy clouds in the sky.

Streams, rivers, oceans and seas,
The best in the world,
Clouds forming into a big one,
It gets bigger, bigger and bigger,
Then it starts to rain.

Air bubbles struggling to get to the top,
Then it starts to hailstone.

That's water!

Eilidh Aldridge (8)
Newton Primary School, Dunblane

A Scottish Soldier

I'm a Scottish soldier
I see men swishing their swords
And battleaxes flung high into the air.
I hear people screaming for help as they sadly die.

I taste blood and sweat, as I fight to the death.
I smell mud squelching underfoot.
I fight for my country.
I'm tired. Exhausted.

I want to stop fighting.

Ciara Dougan (9)
Newton Primary School, Dunblane

Water

Geysers shooting up like a bullet,
Clouds that look like scrunched up paper,
Fog moving gently through the air.

Rivers full of salmon and trout,
Condensation rising up into the atmosphere,
Swamps not flowing, unlike rivers,
Dew hanging off pieces of grass.

Air bubbles trapped in ice cubes,
Hailstones falling and hurting people,
Ice crystals hanging off the trees.

That's water!

Craig Mason (8)
Newton Primary School, Dunblane

Water

Evaporating steam rising into the sky,
Exploding geysers firing steam into the air,
Wet fog making it hard to see,
Fluffy clouds like cotton balls.

Wet dew in the morning on the grass,
Wet water out of the sea,
Crashing waterfalls into rivers.

Cold snowflakes falling from the sky,
Floating icebergs in Antarctica,
Small air bubbles inside ice.

That's water!

Gavin Aikman (8)
Newton Primary School, Dunblane

Water

Dull ugly fog, up in the mountain,
Exploding massive geysers going really fast,
Heavy dark clouds, going to pour,
Light mist down in the valley,
Evaporating steam going higher and higher in the air.

Big whirlpools spinning around,
Calm ponds settling down,
Popping bubbles going away,
Big waves on the sea trying to get to the sand.

Snowflakes falling down gently,
Sharp ice crystals on trees,
Cold snow falling,
Frozen frost on the grass.

That's water!

Gregor Bell (8)
Newton Primary School, Dunblane

I Am A Scottish Soldier

I see a coat of arms,
Powerful, strong,
Well-armed soldiers.

I hear screaming, shouting and dying people,
Squelching mud.

I smell people's blood, steel and metal.

I taste my own tears.

I feel very scared, because I think I'm going to die.

Luke Matthewson (9)
Newton Primary School, Dunblane

Water

Evaporating steam rising and swirling,
Big fluffy clouds floating and rising,
Big scary geysers erupting,
Low fog about rivers,
Lots of mist so cars can't see,
Very hot water vapour, as hot as the sun.

Big dark clouds with rain pouring out,
Big lovely waterfalls spraying,
Blue and green oceans splashing,
Long, thin, calm streams for swimming in,
Big calm rivers with ducks swimming,
Big long lakes, good for swimming.

Small, lovely, cold snowflakes coming from the sky,
Big heavy hailstones hitting people on the head,
Cold snow falling in winter,
Big cold icicles looking like knives.

That's water!

Lucy Darby (8)
Newton Primary School, Dunblane

Water

Fluffy white clouds floating and moving from side to side,
Tall long geysers swirling into the sky,
Boiling steam, burning and rumbling,
Dull fog whirling softly into the sky.

Huge shiny raindrops falling to the floor,
Oceans swishing all around, floating peacefully,
Bubbles popping slowly and turning into a liquid.

Snowflakes falling down, landing on the ground,
Ice cubes melting, melting like crystals.

That's water!

Emily Dickinson (8)
Newton Primary School, Dunblane

Water

Evaporating steam swirling gently up into the sky,
Hot geysers blasting out flaming red-hot steam,
Up into the clear blue sky,
Big white and pink fluffy clouds,
Making the sky colourful and bright,
Hot water vapour swirling up gently,
Up in the atmosphere and out to space.

Liquid bubbles going up into the sky and popping,
Misty condensation steaming up and dripping onto the ground,
Wet water all over the world, keeping us alive,
Calm rivers, green, turquoise, dark blue and light blue,
Swaying gently about.

Small cubes called ice, very cold and made out of water,
Hard hailstones coming down from the sky and bouncing,
Cold frost freezing all the plants, grass and our car.
It might even freeze you!

That's water!

Catriona Ferguson (8)
Newton Primary School, Dunblane

Water

Fluffy mist rising softly,
Swirling round, steaming up windows,
Making them wet.

Fast rivers tearing past
Sweeping past people and
Going down waterfalls.

Hailstones coming down, hitting off the pavement,
Small pieces of ice hitting the roofs.

That's water!

Emma Fitzsimmons (8)
Newton Primary School, Dunblane

Water

Swirling clouds always moving,
Suddenly exploding geysers, always there,
Swirling fog hanging everywhere,
Foggy mist in the bottom of valleys,
Boiling steam always in the atmosphere,
Hot water floating in the air.

Flowing water always moving,
Salty seas, swishing, swashing,
Fast flowing waterfalls, shooting out spray,
Boggy marshes dragging you down,
Little streams trickling down mountainsides.

Icebergs floating in the middle of the oceans,
Hailstones chattering on the windowpanes,
Snowflakes floating down gently,
Frost freezing up the grass.

That's water!

Neil Fraser (8)
Newton Primary School, Dunblane

I Am An Evacuee

I am an evacuee
I feel scared and confused as I wave goodbye.
I feel the fear of everyone around me.
I see the houses that have been bombed.
I hear the people crying as they wave goodbye to their parents.
I wonder if I will be with my brother.
I fear that I might be bombed.

Fraser Wilson (11)
Newton Primary School, Dunblane

Water

Black or white clouds flying high, sometimes fluffy,
Swirling gentle steam comes from a kettle most of the time,
Reminds me of coffee which makes me thirsty,
Noisy big geysers spurting up high, just like a waterfall.

Swirling whirlpools making a loud burp when they're finished,
Sticky soapy bubbles drifting in the air,
Running taps pouring out water.

Cold ice in the freezer, you can see through,
Annoying hailstones looking like sea glass,
Hitting your head,
Small balls of snow making you cold.

That's water!

Iona Grant (8)
Newton Primary School, Dunblane

Water

The flowing clouds are floating in the air,
Unclear fog darkens up in the night,
Evaporating steam rising to environment.

Blown up bubbles in the air,
Floating, shiny rain falling off the roof,
Big waterfalls crashing, banging.

Ice melting very quickly,
Icicles dropping off roofs,
Snowflakes making nice patterns.

That's water!

Rebecca Hay (7)
Newton Primary School, Dunblane

Water

Floating clouds flying up,
Thick mist in your way,
Grey fog moving around,
Steam coming up, turning into water vapour.

Waterfalls come down fast,
Sometimes it meets with the sun,
Making a rainbow,
Condensation on glass,
It goes cold and sometimes we draw on it,
With our fingers.

Air bubbles come up sometimes as it gets frozen,
It comes up like a mountain.

That's how it goes!

Niamh Gilhooly (7)
Newton Primary School, Dunblane

Water

Huge geysers shooting up in the air,
Fluffy mist rising carefully, slowly,
Floating water vapour as hot as the sun.

Flowing rivers, very fast,
Falling waterfall, pouring down,
Swish, water running down my throat.

Melting ice, slippery,
Big icebergs, floating in Antarctic,
Thin icicles, smashing on the ground.

That's water!

Ross Murray (8)
Newton Primary School, Dunblane

Water

It is like fog, mist, very scary,
Very sad and down, clouds are sad
Exploding steam, watch out!
It is just like geysers, a fizzy drink,
When you shake it explodes.

Bubbles look like they have oil in them,
It is like clouds, a pillow,
It is just waterfalls, like rain.

Icicles just like a knife,
Snow very thick and soft,
Ice, just like a brick.

That's water!

Lewis Hardy (8)
Newton Primary School, Dunblane

Water

Huge geysers exploding,
Moving clouds floating,
Evaporating steam rising,
Swirling mist moving gently.

Crashing waves in the ocean,
Early morning dew on the grass,
Falling rain from the clouds.

Icicles dangling from the roof,
Huge icebergs in the sea,
Hailstones falling from the sky.

That's water!

Sam Polatajko (8)
Newton Primary School, Dunblane

In Scotland

In Scotland,
Up the Munroes,
I can see the flowers grow.
I hear the leaves rustle on the trees,
I taste the coolness of the breeze.
I smell the perfume of the wind.

I see the winding River Tay,
I hear the rush of the water each day.
I taste fresh water from the spring,
The river has refreshment to bring.

I see the deer leaping across the stream,
The fox is ready and cunning and keen.
I taste the bacon we have cooked at the campfire,
I smell the smell of Scotland.

Naomi Moodie (8)
North Muirton Primary School, Perth

No November!

No more sun
No more fun
No more beaches
No more rosy cheeks
No more heat
No more summers
No more long days
No more playing outside
No more sand
No more outside days
No more outside games
No more buckets and spades
No November!

Erin Williams (10)
North Muirton Primary School, Perth

Poppies For Peace

Blood-red poppies grow in fields
Under crosses row by row
Hear the explosion of the bombs shrieking,
Falling from the sky.
Listen to the rumbling echo in the trenches where they die.
Soldiers falling heap on heap.
Risking their lives for you and I.
In Flanders, now you know the story that happened
Long, long ago.

Lyndsey Christie (10)
North Muirton Primary School, Perth

Cheese - Impossibilities

Races in the mature racer.

Mows the lawn with his cheddar shredder.

He has cheesy feet.

Has a friend called Mac (Mac and Cheese)?

Hates doughnuts - only eats the hole.

Lost his dad to a sandwich.

Ross Moffat (10)
North Muirton Primary School, Perth

Poppies

The poppies help remind us of fighters that fought
And gracefully died.
Guns blazed every minute
But thousands died every second.
There was shouting, screaming, screeching and
Blazing too.
So remember everyone who lost their lives for us.

Ryan Blake (10)
North Muirton Primary School, Perth

In Scotland

I see trees, crows, grass and clouds.
I hear birds tweeting. And I can hear the River Tay.
I taste the haggis going into my mouth.
I smell the lovely flowers around me.
I see rabbits and deer and lots of other animals staring at me from above.
I see the River Tay flowing.
I see fish in the river, colourful fish.
I see the sun shining in my eyes.
I see other human beings.
The people wave at me so I wave back.
They ask me if I am enjoying my haggis, so I reply yes,
Then they tell me to make sure that I don't get too fat.
They laugh and so do I and they go away.
I hear cows going moo,
I hear sheep going baa, I hear, see, taste and smell lots of things,
But the most important thing of all is that I can see Scotland.

Cody Nicholson (8)
North Muirton Primary School, Perth

Poppies

When our fellow soldiers died
Blood-red poppies rose.
When the noise became peace.
After the sergeant stopped shouting.
Across those Flanders fields.
And the bombs stopped whistling in the wind.
The sun shone on the flowers.
Not on shotguns and bayonets
Flashing in the sunshine.
Those people died in pain so far away for us to see.
Their sacrifice was made just for you and me.

Lewis Robertson (10)
North Muirton Primary School, Perth

No November

No football in the sunny park.
No bikes to play round the street.
No summer holidays to look forward to.
No more cars for Sunday, sunny picnics.
No ice cream to melt on my chin.
No swimming at the beach in trunks.
No bright night.
No bright days.
No sunbathing.
No more suncream, sunglasses or hat.
No November!

Liam McInnes (10)
North Muirton Primary School, Perth

Poppies

Remember the peace in Flanders field
Enemies bomb and bullets fly
Men will die in Flanders field
Everyone fought for their country
Many will sacrifice their lives
Even their ages
Mothers will cry one single tear
We will remember them.

Louize Clark (10)
North Muirton Primary School, Perth

Poppies

Poppies grow in Flanders fields
Remind us of red, red blood
We sit at home with hope and fear
Two million people died that year
Who sacrificed their lives for us
We will remember them!

Charley Gannon (9)
North Muirton Primary School, Perth

Poppies Grow

Poppies grow in Flanders field.
The birds sing scarcely above.
Flanders field full of bombs and flying bullets
Where people risked their lives for us to live in peace.
Blasting bombs and blooming blood-red poppies burst
From the trenches.
So remember us as the years go by.
Remember, always wear a poppy to appreciate
What we did for you.

Jimmy Townsley (10)
North Muirton Primary School, Perth

Poppies

P oppies blooming in Flanders Field
O h what can we do?
P oppies, we will remember them all
P oppies remind us of everyone that died.
I hate the sight of their lost blood.
E very gunshot, they all died.
S ome people might think it's stupid, but people do die in wars.

Rachel Dickson (10)
North Muirton Primary School, Perth

Malawi

Malawi looks sandy, dusty and dry with its scorching sun
And ramshackle huts.
Malawi feels like soft, dry sand falling through my fingers.
Malawi sounds like children playing in the school.
Malawi smells like all the fresh fish in the market
And people sweating.
Malawi tastes sweet like the sugar cane.

Peter Gillson (10)
Pirnmill Primary School, Isle of Arran

Malawi

Malawi looks like the golden sun reflecting on the crystal clear
Lake's surface.
Malawi feels like soft grains of sand running through your hands.
Malawi sounds like children running and screaming to school.
Malawi smells of food you see at the market.
Malawi has the sweet taste of sugar cane dissolving on your tongue.

Hannah Ross (11)
Pirnmill Primary School, Isle of Arran

Malawi

Malawi looks like small mud houses.
Malawi feels like lumpy and sloppy mud.
Malawi sounds like twirping birds and roaring hippos.
Malawi smells like smelly fish in a market and
People selling scented spices.
Malawi tastes sweet like sugary sugar cane.

Sam Sneddon (10)
Pirnmill Primary School, Isle of Arran

Malawi

Malawi looks like a very poor country.
Malawi feels gritty.
Malawi sounds like horses running.
Malawi smells like dirt.
Malawi tastes like sugar cane.

Gregor Stewart (9)
Pirnmill Primary School, Isle of Arran

Malawi

Malawi tastes like a sweet sweet sugar cane.
Malawi looks like smiling faces.
Malawi feels like soft sand running through your hands.
Malawi sounds like loudly roaring hippos and it smells like lots of Spices.

Duncan Ross (9)
Pirnmill Primary School, Isle of Arran

Malawi

Malawi looks like a dry and sandy place.
Malawi feels like rough oven baked mud brick houses.
Malawi sounds like laughing happy children.
Malawi smells like fresh fish and tasty yams in the markets.
Malawi tastes like sugary sugar cane.

Iain Logan (10)
Pirnmill Primary School, Isle of Arran

Little Brown Bat - Cinquain

Brown bats
Flying around
Hunting, catching, eating
Always tasting such lovely food
Brown bat.

Liam Grant (11)
Pitcairn Primary School, Almondbank

Bats!

Bats are frantic, furry, friendly things,
Always flapping their tiny wings.

Among the caves, in the night,
Can't see anything with that sight!

Eating spiders, beetles, flies,
Catching anything if close by.

Echolocation comes in handy
Not unless there is some candy.

Among the trees it likes to get fit
But not that funny, the cat gets it!

Kieran Smith (11)
Pitcairn Primary School, Almondbank

The Innocent

Newly born with a coat of silk,
Feeding off its mother's milk.

A harmless face of innocence,
How could men be so careless?

To think this little winged mouse
Would be labelled scary or dangerous.

What harm has it done to us?
Why should this creature cause a fuss?

So next time you see one, do not scream,
They're not as scary as they seem!

Shelley Hobson (10)
Pitcairn Primary School, Almondbank

Small Bats

S mall bats are sometimes cute
M y old house had bats in the attic
A ll bats are mammals
L arge bats are scary
L ittle bats only weigh about five to ten grams.

B ats only come out at night
A nd bats use echolocation
T o find their way about
S ometimes you will see bats out at night.

Jodie McDonald (10)
Pitcairn Primary School, Almondbank

Bats

Bats wake up at the start of night
Go looking for food wing the power of flight
Soaring about using echolocation,
Finding prey without losing temptation.
In the winter it hibernates,
While staying with its bat mates,
It wakes up at the start of spring,
Feeling like a queen or king.

Ben Millar (11)
Pitcairn Primary School, Almondbank

The Bat

Creepy, scary, horrendous things,
Clammy dirty flying wings,
Then I met a little bat,
The cutest thing I've ever seen
As smooth as silk
As warm as milk
Now I love bats.

Jennifer McGregor (11)
Pitcairn Primary School, Almondbank

A Bat's Life

Bats are strange little creatures,
They have very weird features,
Bats like to fly around at night,
If you see one, you'll get a fright!

Some are black, some are brown,
Some look like they have a frown,
Some are slim, some are fat,
There are lots of features to a bat!

There are different species in different places,
All have very different faces,
With their long ears and piggy nose,
And the sharp claws on their toes!

Watch them fly as they swoop away
Going to sleep for another day,
Diving around in the sky,
It must be really great to fly . . .

Leah Panton (11)
Pitcairn Primary School, Almondbank

A Little Bat

I see a little bat
That's nothing like a rat
It's cousin to the mouse
They both nest in your house
Those strange little creatures
With funny little features
Those funny little things
Make hats with their wings
It flies about through the air
Mum gets scared in case it lands in her hair
I think it's time to rest my head
But you're just getting out of bed.

Jodie Sutherland (11)
Pitcairn Primary School, Almondbank

Creepy Creatures!

Aww little bats *sooo* short and stout,
The way you wiggle your little snouts,
Piggy nose and stick-up ears,
Oh how you make some people cheer!
'I know that you come out at night,
And yes you give little ones a fright,
It's just because you're dark as night'
And swooping whilst you are in flight,
To catch some food for you to eat,
Night-night bats it's time for sleep!

Kirstie Robertson (11)
Pitcairn Primary School, Almondbank

Bat Poem

I thought that bats were birds
Now I know that bats are mammals.

When I was wee,
I thought that bats were going to bang into me.

But now I know what echolocation does
It makes bats not bang into stuff.

Now I have a black, furry, small friend
I will love it to the end.

Andrew Parker (10)
Pitcairn Primary School, Almondbank

Bats - Cinquain

Cool bats
Flying, swooping
Gliding, catching midges
In the night sky, dodging objects
Bats rock!

Kieran Duff (11)
Pitcairn Primary School, Almondbank

The Blitz

The Blitz to most seemed like the end
To some the end was just round the bend.

The evacuees were leaving fast
And all around the big bombs blast.

Zoe Donnachy (11)
St Mun's Primary School, Dunoon

Hedgehog

Hedgehog
Prickly, spiky,
Slow, quiet, shuffly,
Cool, happy, confused, shivery,
Hibernates.

Jamie Dominick (11)
St Mun's Primary School, Dunoon

Leaves

Leaves
Brown, crispy,
Soaring, frightened, falling,
Sad, mad, scared, hurt,
Dead.

Eleanor Donovan (11)
St Mun's Primary School, Dunoon

Leaves - Haiku

Coloured autumn leaves
Dancing in the autumn wind
All day and night long.

Rianne Emmerson (11)
St Mun's Primary School, Dunoon

The Blitz

I'm a young boy in the Blitz,
Why am I caught up in this?
It's really quite scary
I'm looking for my mother, Mary
She's not home
I'm all alone,
I should be playing with a friend
Not watching the world end.
The Germans are bombing, we're not ready
I'm so scared, I wish I had my teddy.

Graeme Brown (11)
St Mun's Primary School, Dunoon

The Badger

Badger
Hairy, scary
Black and white
Cool, quiet, sad, lonely,
Autumn.

Colin Wheatley (10)
St Mun's Primary School, Dunoon

Leaves

Leaves,
Crumbly, crunchy,
Prancing, soaring, gliding,
Frightened, cold, scared, hurt,
Dancer.

Liam Glancy (10)
St Mun's Primary School, Dunoon

Autumn

Autumn
Cold, windy,
Leaves are falling
Waiting, happy and cool
Winter.

Michael Hagan (11)
St Mun's Primary School, Dunoon

Leaves

Leaves,
Crunchy, crumbly,
Swaying, falling, blowing
Sad, angry, unhappy, cold,
Skeleton.

Liam Jack (11)
St Mun's Primary School, Dunoon

The Rose - Haiku

I give you this rose
Treasure it with all your heart
It's my soul and life.

Zara Collings (11)
St Mun's Primary School, Dunoon

Me! - Haiku

Riona Stewart
Very cool and fantastic
Amazingly smart.

Riona Stewart (11)
St Mun's Primary School, Dunoon

Autumn

Autumn
Crunchy leaves
Falling, tumbling, moulding,
Sad, cold, hurt, scared,
Winter.

Siobhan Cartwright (11)
St Mun's Primary School, Dunoon

Hallowe'en

Hallowe'en
Fun, creepy
Strangers giving candy
Spooky, silly, scary, enjoyable
Celebration.

Hannah Cruickshank (11)
St Mun's Primary School, Dunoon

Squirrels

Squirrels
Red, hairy
Fast, eat nuts
Busy, scared, mad, crazy
Endangered.

Derrick McPhee (11)
St Mun's Primary School, Dunoon

Hallowe'en

Hallowe'en is almost here
I'll be dressed up in my gear
Knocking doors it's hit and miss
But I'll be there with my big fist
A song, a joke, an act, a dance,
Will surely win an applause of hands
I can't wait till that big night,
To give all of Greenock a massive fright.

Chloe Canning (10)
St Patrick's Primary School, Greenock

My Dog

I have a young dog called Mac,
He is such a pain in the back,
His barking is like old Tom next door,
His fleas are jumping all over the floor,
At night when he's smelly he sleeps on my bed,
And he runs at me every day to lick my head.
I can't wait till he is fed.

Brendan McEleny (10)
St Patrick's Primary School, Greenock

Pat

There was an old man called Pat
Who had a pet rat called Nat
He came out of his cage
Drove Pat to a rage
And that was the end of the rat called Nat.

Jamie Jenkins (10)
St Patrick's Primary School, Greenock

If Children Ruled The World

If children ruled the world
I would be the captain of the navy ship
And teachers would be slaves
Girls' shops would be banned
Toys would be free
The schools would be amusement parks
And Hallowe'en would be called 'Funnyween'
Christmas would be called 'Presentmas'
It would be good if children ruled the
World!

Kieran Hopkin (8)
St Patrick's Primary School, Greenock

Silence

S hh! Don't wake the baby
I t's just newly born
L ying in its cot upstairs
E xhausted parents are having a rest
N ervous that the baby will wake up
C rying for them
E verybody knows how hard it is having a baby - but especially them!

Gregor Black (9)
St Patrick's Primary School, Greenock

Joy

Joy is yellow
It smells like freshly cut grass
And feels like my soft pillow
Joy tastes like a bit of cake
Joy looks like a garden of flowers
And sounds like the bluebirds singing.

Louise Middleton (9)
St Patrick's Primary School, Greenock

If Children Ruled The World

If children ruled the world
Parents would be put to bed at 2 o'clock in the afternoon
And we will party all night.

Sweeties are good for you and fruit and vegetables are for wimps
If only we ruled the world.

If children ruled the world
There would be no more pollution,
No more hunting and no more pain.

Lucy Jackson (9)
St Patrick's Primary School, Greenock

My Cat

I had a cat both black and white,
He used to sleep in a sack at night
One awful evening a dog came around
And my poor cat was stuck to the ground.
He wriggled and wriggled all over the mat
And that was the end of my black and white cat.

Hannah Blue (9)
St Patrick's Primary School, Greenock

Anger

Anger is crimson
It tastes like acid
It smells like the consuming fumes of smoke
I looks like the burning rage of a wild fire
It sounds like the catastrophic boom of a volcano erupting
It feels like a third degree burn.

Kieran Wylie (10)
St Patrick's Primary School, Greenock

The Crazy Zoo

There's a place in the world
Where animals change sound
From all the other animals
Here's how different they are.

The grizzly, growling gorilla tweets
And the lazy, lying-down-all-day lion miaows
The underwater whale has feet
And the fish start to dance to 70s music.

The tricky, tearing-things tiger barks,
The eggy elegant elephant roars,
The giant gooey giraffe blows bubbles
If you had this zoo you would never get bored.

Now you know how weird this zoo is,
Do you really want to go there?
I can't stand it, I really do hate it
Even though my mum wants to go every year.

Oh no! We're going tomorrow!

Megan Dougan (10)
St Patrick's Primary School, Greenock

Random Pudding

Random pudding, random pudding
I love pudding, yes I do
Chocolate ones, creamy ones and minty ones first
I love pudding, yes I do
I could eat it until I burst
I love pudding, yes I do
Thin ones, fat ones and random puddings too!

Lewis Murray (10)
St Patrick's Primary School, Greenock

Autumn

Autumn is tropical like a beautiful beach
It sounds like leaves dancing at my feet
It tastes like amazing cherries fresh from a tree
When all the colours fly to me
It smells like the damp ground with leaves swirling all about
It looks like leaves surrounding my cold feet
It feels like wind blowing down my body
It reminds me of the skies of blue when all the colours say goodbye to you.

Dayna Reid (8)
St Patrick's Primary School, Greenock

School

School is for learning but not for fun
So come on let's go everyone
We'll go there to play
Perhaps even stay
Oh no! What's that? Reading, writing, no fun
Come on everybody, let's go, let's run!

Kaitlynne Cannon (10)
St Patrick's Primary School, Greenock

Football

Football, football you are great!
Some people love, some people hate.
Some teams are good, some teams are bad,
But the team that loses is always sad.

Daniel Orr (10)
St Patrick's Primary School, Greenock

If Children Ruled The World

If children ruled the world,
Everything would be chocolate.
Chocolate buildings, chocolate huts,
Even chocolate squirrel's nuts.

If children ruled the world,
Kittens would roam the streets,
And every day, even at school,
I'd have a kitten to meet!

If children ruled the world,
We could stay up late!
We could have a party,
And find a new mate!

Amy Doak (9)
St Patrick's Primary School, Greenock

Apple Pie

I love apple pie
It's very, very good
I love apple pie,
It's my favourite food!

I love apple pie,
The crust all golden and brown
I love apple pie
It's better than a shiny crown!

I love apple pie,
With thick double cream,
I love apple pie,
I think about it in my dreams!

Leah McCluskey (10)
St Patrick's Primary School, Greenock

If Children Ruled The World

If children ruled the world
We would own the QE2.
We would hang around in the pool all day.
I would like to be a queen too.

If children ruled the world
I would have super powers.
I would stop the killing of people and animals.
I would do that for 1 or 2 hours.

If children ruled the world
We would like to get our way.
It's unjust, it's always Mum and Dad's way.
All I ask is just one day.

Erin Leith (9)
St Patrick's Primary School, Greenock

If Children Ruled The World

If children ruled the world
They would be billionaires
They would own the entire city
And have a snow machine in the playground.

If children ruled the world
They would be invisible
And everything would be chocolate
And we'd rule the adults.

If children ruled the world
There would be no smoking or drugs
And no illness.

Marc Lapsley (8)
St Patrick's Primary School, Greenock

Autumn

Autumn is blue like the deep sea shining with dolphins jumping
from it.
The high winds sound like waves crashing against the shore.
It tastes like hot chocolate with marshmallow on a cold, dark, night.
It smells like damp soggy leaves on the ground.
It looks like a colourful rainbow on the hard, damp ground.
It feels like a brown prickly hedgehog gathering its food
When it's ready to hibernate.
It reminds me of bare brown trees with no more leaves on them.

Matthew Burns (8)
St Patrick's Primary School, Greenock

Autumn

Autumn is red like our sparkling heart inside of us.
It sounds like flames of a bonfire snapping and crackling.
It tastes like strawberry jam on your hot toast in the morning.
It smells like hot chocolate in the cold evening.
It looks like a colourful rainbow in your garden.
It feels like a mother fox cuddling her baby.
It reminds me of spring flowers, all different colours,
Just around the corner.

Erin Watt (8)
St Patrick's Primary School, Greenock

Autumn

Autumn is red like the leaves blowing in the sky.
It sounds like the leaves swishing around.
It tastes like warm toast I have in my bed.
It smells like the dew in the grass in my garden.
It looks like the shiny star in the sky.
It feels like cold, damp leaves on the ground.
It reminds me of the Red Arrows shooting out trails of colour.

Nicole Kangley (8)
St Patrick's Primary School, Greenock

Autumn

Autumn is red like a glittery heart beating inside of me.
It sounds like a bonfire crackling and crunching at night.
It tastes like a cherry tomato showered under cold water.
It smells like a cupcake covered in sprinkles.
It looks like an icy car on Christmas Eve.
It feels like a grey rabbit curling up in a ball.
It reminds me of all sorts of colours of autumn-red,
orange, gold and brown.

Amy Leith (7)
St Patrick's Primary School, Greenock

Autumn

Autumn is red like a shimmering heart beating.
It sounds like leaves falling and twirling to the ground.
It tastes like a lovely cup of tea with a chestnut.
It smells like a lovely scented candle burning,
Dancing and twirling at night.
It looks like a beautiful tree with lots of colours.
It feels like a lovely crisp autumn morning.
It reminds me of my mum's home-made soup.

Eve Paterson (8)
St Patrick's Primary School, Greenock

The Witch's Brew

In goes worms, spiders and glue
Birds, frogs and an old smelly shoe
Beetles and snails and *oops!*
The old black cat
These all go in to make the witch's brew.
Except the cat of course!

Caitlin Monaghan (10)
St Patrick's Primary School, Greenock

Autumn

Awesome brown trees,
Swaying with the wind.

Fiery red leaves
Falling and dying.

The morning is wet and misty,
The people are having fun.

On a pitch-black night
The nights are getting longer.

Stephen McShane (11)
St Patrick's Primary School, Greenock

Autumn

Big green trees,
Dancing and prancing.

Bright red leaves,
Falling and blowing away.

Dark scary nights,
Cold and windy.

And autumn is just beginning.

Dylan Maloney (10)
St Patrick's Primary School, Greenock

Autumn

Beautiful red trees,
Fabulous and golden.

Falling red leaves,
Blowing around and crunching.

Cold and misty weather,
And this is my favourite season.

Rebecca Maunders (10)
St Patrick's Primary School, Greenock

Autumn

Beautiful yellow trees,
Waving and swooshing.

Shiny golden leaves,
Colourful and crunchy.

Very dark nights,
Cold and scary.

And that is what autumn is like.

Justin Bowie (10)
St Patrick's Primary School, Greenock

Autumn

Brightly coloured trees,
Dancing and swaying.

Fiery red leaves,
Falling and spreading.

Dark misty nights,
Cold and frosty.

Autumn is here for now!

Shannon Kangley (11)
St Patrick's Primary School, Greenock

Autumn

Golden fabulous leaves,
Terrific and wonderful.

Reddish-brown leaves,
Falling and scattering.

Pitch-black nights,
Cold and misty.

This is the view of my autumn.

Lauren Renfrew (11)
St Patrick's Primary School, Greenock

Autumn

Enchanting bright trees,
Dancing and prancing.

Rich and golden,
Dropping and blowing away.

Dark looking nights,
Icy and foggy.

That is my autumn.

Ryan Campbell (10)
St Patrick's Primary School, Greenock

Autumn

Tall golden trees,
Dancing and swaying.
Fiery red leaves,
Falling and floating through the air.
Dark, peaceful nights,
Starry and misty.
Autumn is a beautiful time of year.

Jacqueline Pye (11)
St Patrick's Primary School, Greenock

Autumn

Great brown trees,
Swaying and swishing.
Golden and crackling leaves,
Crispy and crunching.
Frosty dark nights,
Cold and long.
This is my view of autumn.

Jack Harrington (11)
St Patrick's Primary School, Greenock

Autumn

Beautiful tall trees,
Dancing and prancing.

Crunchy golden leaves,
Still and noisy.

Pitch-black nights,
Cold and frosty.

And autumn is just beginning.

Kelly Fox (11)
St Patrick's Primary School, Greenock

Autumn

Beautiful brown trees,
Looming and fabulous.

Beautiful golden leaves
Falling and sparkling.

Dark frosty nights
Cold and misty
And this is my view of autumn.

Ainsley McGovern (11)
St Patrick's Primary School, Greenock

Autumn

Beautiful golden trees,
Looming high and tall.

Bright orange leaves,
Drooping slowly to the ground.

Dark, frosty nights,
Cold and misty.

This is how I feel about autumn.

Nicole Laughlan (11)
St Patrick's Primary School, Greenock

Autumn

Amazing golden trees,
Dancing and prancing.

Fiery red leaves,
Falling down onto the ground.

The mornings are wet and misty,
The children are having fun.

On a pitch-black autumn night
It is time to say, 'Goodnight.'

Karly Balloch (11)
St Patrick's Primary School, Greenock

Autumn

Spectacular old trees,
Prancing and dancing.

Beautiful golden leaves,
Falling and scattering to the ground.

Dark frosty nights,
Cold and fabulous.
I love autumn!

Sarah Clark (10)
St Patrick's Primary School, Greenock

Autumn

Wonderful, terrific trees
Prancing and dancing
Glittering golden leaves
Falling and blowing away
Dark, cold nights
Frosty and cool
This all happens in autumn.

Declan Hughes (11)
St Patrick's Primary School, Greenock

Autumn

Wonderful red trees,
Graceful and glorious.

Yellow golden leaves,
Scattering and blowing away.

Jet-black nights,
Freezing and foggy.

And autumn is now!

Ryan Smyth (11)
St Patrick's Primary School, Greenock

Autumn

Lots of trees,
Brilliant and tall.
Amazing red leaves,
Gleaming and golden.
Misty black nights,
Cold and windy,
Autumn is so much fun.

Amy Farren (11)
St Patrick's Primary School, Greenock

Autumn

Wonderful brown trees,
Fabulous and colourful.

Golden brown leaves,
Cracking and falling.

Very dark nights,
Frosty and misty.

This is a lovely autumn day.

Becky Carr (11)
St Patrick's Primary School, Greenock

If Children Ruled The World

If children ruled the world,
There would be no drugs or any roads.
What there would be is floating schools
And flying motorbikes that lead you up to the school.

If children ruled the world,
It would be your birthday every day
And every country would be named after you.
Wouldn't that be great!
No more pollution, yes, that's what I'd do.

If children ruled the world
No more extinction or anything of the sort.
No not that.
No more bad people.
Oh no, not in my world.

Cara O'Donnell (9)
St Patrick's Primary School, Greenock

If Children Ruled The World

If I ruled the world
I would get parents to bed sharp
And they would buy me Australia.

If I ruled the world
I would ban smoking
We don't want to choke
I would ban drunk drivers
Because you could crash.

If I ruled the world
I would party all day
I would invite people everywhere
Only if I ruled the world.

Rachael Phanco (9)
St Patrick's Primary School, Greenock

If Children Ruled The World

If children ruled the world
There would be fizzy drinks and no dentists to stop the sweets
And we'd never brush our teeth.

If children ruled the world
Hallowe'en would be every day
And birthdays every week
And Christmas once a month.

If children ruled the world
There would be no homework or school work
Because the school would have been blown up.

If children ruled the world
Swimming would be free
The toys and pets would all be mine
If only children ruled the world.

Shona Moran (8)
St Patrick's Primary School, Greenock

If Children Ruled The World

If children ruled the world
Money would grow on trees
And everything would be free.

If children ruled the world
I would be queen
And own everything.

If children ruled the world
Girls would be royal
And boys would be slaves.

If children ruled the world
It would snow all year round
I could own an igloo
That was worthwhile.

Anna Traynor (8)
St Patrick's Primary School, Greenock

Autumn

Autumn is red like delicious strawberry juice
gleaming in a silver glass.
It sounds like the wind swirling round in the beautiful bright blue sky.
It tastes like delicious home-made soup with crunchy bread
waiting for me when I get home from school.
It smells like the damp colourful leaves on the bright green grass.
It looks like millions of leaves scattering and mashing on the damp
concrete ground.
It feels like the soft crunchy leaves blowing on the shimmering
autumn ground.
It reminds me of the sunset that shimmers in the autumn breeze.

Jasmine Barrie (8)
St Patrick's Primary School, Greenock

My World

Inside my head I've got a world
World with candyfloss clouds and chocolate cookie ground
Strawberry houses with ice cream cone trees
Chocolate rivers and marshmallow seas
And liquorice cars
Argh! That's my world.

Shannon O'Neill (10)
St Patrick's Primary School, Greenock

My Holiday

My holiday is the colours blue and white.
It tastes like ice cream and hot dogs.
It smells like butter popcorn and candy apples.
It looks like parades and roller coasters and sunshine every day.
It sounds like fireworks and happy songs and dolphins splashing.
My holiday feels like a dream come true.

Mark McLachlan (8)
St Patrick's Primary School, Greenock

If Children Ruled The World

If children ruled the world
Bad food would be good
And I would have as much sweets as I want
I would also blow up all the schools.

I would make everybody Celtic supporters
I would make school banned for children,
Homework too.
I would make very deep snow every day.

I would also make a school for teachers.

Courtney Stanton (9)
St Patrick's Primary School, Greenock

If Children Ruled The World

If children ruled the world!
I would stop killing animals.
If children ruled the world
I would own the QE2.
I would be in the pool . . . *cooool!*
I would love it if there was no homework.
If children ruled the world
I would stop smoking and drugs.

Amy Leith (8)
St Patrick's Primary School, Greenock

An Old Granny

There was an old granny called Betty
Who loved to eat lots of spaghetti
She ate a lot
Straight out of the pot
And now she is known as Big Betty.

Stephanie Owens (9)
St Patrick's Primary School, Greenock

The Wind

Anger
A wild roar breaks from the night,
People look to see the caller,
But he's not in sight.

Thrashing and bashing,
A gate's sent crashing,
The wind's a mallet,
Mashing the trees,
With experienced ease.

Calming
The anger's subsiding,
Slowly, gradually becoming a chink,
Wait it's back,
It's on the brink.

Gone
It's gone,
The silence is like death,
Everyone comes and draws
A breath,
The wind watches,
Silent tears drip from his cheeks,
All he wants is a hug,
To be loved and snug,
Everyone runs away,
Not me, I will stay.

Rose Richmond (10)
Skipness Primary School, Skipness

Our New Baby

Our new baby
Is coming home
Today.
I can't wait till the baby
Comes home!

His name is
Finlay James Campbell
Vischer.
I can't wait till the baby
Comes home!

Mummy and Daddy
Tell me he has
Dark brown hair.
I can't wait till the baby
Comes home!

I'll cuddle him,
Love him and
Help to bath him.
I can't wait till the baby
Comes home.

Megan Vischer (7)
Skipness Primary School, Skipness

When I Was Ill

Came back from Rose's
Feeling ill,
Went to the doctor's
And got a pill.
Skipped school for five days running,
At home doing nothing.

All those days I lay on the couch,
Moaning ouch,
Reading a word or two,
Dozing off and feeling blue.
Mum said I looked red,
So I should stay in bed.
Till the very end,
So I would mend.
Wearing my jim-jams every day,
Not caring what people would say.

Now I'm here,
Back in school,
Writing this poem for you.

Hannah Prill (10)
Skipness Primary School, Skipness

Around The Sun

Around the sun, around the stars
Around the planets including Mars
Around the water, around the land
Around the moon and the sand
Around the cold and the hot
Around Jupiter and its spot
Around the future and the past
Around the sun with a blast!

Callum White (10)
Tomnacross Primary School, Kiltarlity

The Eagle's Working Hard

The eagle's working hard
To wake her little ones,
The eagle's working hard
To listen out for guns.

The eagle's working hard
To find some juicy prey,
The eagle's working hard
To end the long hard day.

Hannah Farman (10)
Tomnacross Primary School, Kiltarlity

Friends

Friends can help you when you're hurt
They cheer you up when you're down
They play with you when no one will
They help you through rough times
That's what makes a friend.

Dylan Johnston (10)
Tomnacross Primary School, Kiltarlity

My Grandad

My grandad went away to war
To fight a war on another shore
And on that shore he fought for peace
To save our lives
And I will remember him.

Rhunne Cassels-MacGregor (10)
Tomnacross Primary School, Kiltarlity

Alone

As I parted from there
With nobody to care
Alone, alone, alone.

Floating up high
Nearly touching the sky
Alone, alone, alone.

I'm falling down low
With nowhere to go
Alone, alone, alone.

I'm lying on the ground
Never to be found
Alone, alone, alone.

Emma MacRae (11)
Tomnacross Primary School, Kiltarlity

Music

Music all around me
Music in the air
Music makes me want to dance
Music everywhere.

Nikki Mainland (11)
Tomnacross Primary School, Kiltarlity

Horses

They gallop through the trees
Their tails wave in the breeze
Cantering is fun
Good for everyone.

Alex Farquharson (10)
Tomnacross Primary School, Kiltarlity

Beside The Sea

The waves are splashing
The dogs are barking
The seagulls are squawking
As I am playing.

Emily Wilton (10)
Tomnacross Primary School, Kiltarlity

For Allyson

A llyson is my best friend forever,
L ively and fun whatever the weather,
L aughing and joking, we're always together,
Y es, like I said, we're best friends forever.
S leepovers with Allyson are so much fun,
O n these nights we stay up till the sun.
N ow there's one more thing I would like to say
Very best friends
We will always stay.

Lauren Thwaite (11)
Wallace Hall Primary School, Thornhill

Boats

Wave blaster
big boats and small
fast boats in the air
engine whirling in the water
playing out today
scaring fish away
Splashes coming from the water
racing others out there.

Sam Murphy (8)
Wallace Primary School, Elderslie

Dolphin Kennings

Wave rider
Reef hider
Seashell player
Fish eater
Seaweed swisher
Shark avoider
Boat follower
Click communicator
Shrimp finder
Shipwreck explorer
Mermaid carer
Submarine searcher.

Yana Petticrew (8)
Wallace Primary School, Elderslie

The Dolphin Kennings

Wave splasher
Reef searcher
Seaweed hider
Boat player
Ship wrecker
Submarine chaser
Seashell seeker
Click maker
Shrimp eater
Fish finder
Shark sorcerer
Mermaid follower!

Zara Craig (8)
Wallace Primary School, Elderslie

Aliens Kennings

Planet seeker
Slime leaver
Martian eater
Rocket destroyer
Astronaut sinker
Moon searcher
Star minder
Night walker
Human liker
City killer
Ray-gun maker
Flying saucer builder.

Ian Wylie (7)
Wallace Primary School, Elderslie

Alien Kennings

Planet destroyer
Moon blaster
Star looker
Slime shooter
City taker
Night watcher
Human eater
Rocket starter
Ray gun raider
Martian lover
Astronaut disliker
Flying saucer pilot.

Kirsty Wilson (7)
Wallace Primary School, Elderslie

Worms Kennings

Mud swayer
Garden lover
Grass jungle
Bird watcher
Fish food
Slug eater
Ladybird friend
Wormhole maker
Baby spider finder
Rain dancer
Grass climber
Fly eater.

Alannah Ferguson (8)
Wallace Primary School, Elderslie

Aliens Kennings

Human vaporiser
UFO spinner
City raider
Star shiner
Rocket rider
Martian minion
Planet seeker
Nigh chaser
Astronaut ambusher
Moon finder
Universe destroyer
Laser shooter.

Jason Crawford-McElhinney (8)
Wallace Primary School, Elderslie

Dolphin Kennings

Seaweed swayer
Fish eater
Seashell player
Boat finder
Wave jumper
Shipwreck explorer
Shark frightener
Mermaid chaser
Submarine looker
Reef swisher
Shrimp catcher
Water diver.

Iona Gray (8)
Wallace Primary School, Elderslie

Alien Kennings

Planet panicker
Slime soaker
Martian maker
Rocket destroyer
Astronaut eater
Moon minder
Star chaser
Night seeker
Human abductor
City destroyer
Ray gun blaster
Flying saucer expert.

Jamie Smith (8)
Wallace Primary School, Elderslie

Dolphin Kennings

Fish finder
Seaweed swimmer
Boat follower
Wave jumper
Seashell cracker
Mermaid lover
Shipwreck explorer
Shark chaser
Submarine mover
Reef player
Shrimp finder
Click maker.

Lorin Mullen (8)
Wallace Primary School, Elderslie

Recipe For A Dog

Take two floppy ears
Then take four legs and a body
Add some gold as a necklace
Stir in a stubby tail as stubby as a pen lid
Decorate with painted stones for eyes
And you have made a dog.

Paul Kearnan (9)
Whitfield Primary School, Dundee

The Magic Box

(Based on 'Magic Box' by Kit Wright)

I will put in the box . . .

The touch of hair that has been brushed.
The Great Wall of China big and beautiful.
The first mermaid of the Atlantic Ocean.

I will put in the box . . .

The smell of chocolate that has just been melted.
A golden snitch of Harry Potter.
A swan sitting across the shimmering water on a starry night.

My box is made from . . .

A magical glass,
Polka dots from multicoloured glass
And never-melted ice for the hinges.

In my box I will go to the Great Wall of China.

Katie Love (10)
Williamston Primary School, Murieston

My Magic Box

(Based on 'Magic Box' by Kit Wright)

I will put in my box . . .

The rustling of leaves while running down a hill,
A small boy scrambling up a tree,
The feeling of me patting my head.

I will put in my box . . .

The smashing of the ice on the walls,
The taste of sweets in my mouth,
A sea lion jumping over a boat.

I will put in my box . . .

Seeing my dad again,
My grandad sitting beside me again
And my cousin seeing her dad again.

Christopher Govan (10)
Williamston Primary School, Murieston

My Magic Box

(Based on 'Magic Box' by Kit Wright)

I will put in my box . . .

The wind in my face as I ride my white horse through the woods,
The shouting of children playing in the field,
A brush stroking beautiful soft hair.

I will put in my box . . .

The crunching noise of the snow squeezing together to make a ball,
The salty smell of the sea while I make a sandcastle at the beach,
A crab walking across the warm sand.

I will put in my box . . .

The funniest joke of my dad,
My nanny's biggest hugs,
And my brother getting married when he is older.

I will put in my box . . .

A year full of Christmas,
A princess with an electric guitar
And a rock star in a tower.

My box is made from gold, rubies and emeralds
With hearts on the lid and love in the corners.
The hinges are the wings of butterflies.

I shall ride in my box . . .

Through great forests with my favourite rider Pippa Funnel,
And I will go on famous riding shows all around the world.
I will end up lying on a cloud softer than a hundred feathers.

Fiona Howells (10)
Williamston Primary School, Murieston

My Magic Box

(Based on 'Magic Box' by Kit Wright)

I will put in the box . . .

Lying on my trampoline, looking at the beautiful blue sky
and white clouds,
Going to an Indian restaurant and gobbling curry,
The sound of myself singing.

I will put in the box . . .

Building a gigantic snowman,
Swimming in a massive pool in Spain,
Climbing the beautiful mountain in Spain.

I will put in the box . . .

My dad's big bald head,
Giving Gran Yvonne a big hug,
My baby cousin Rhona giving me a big hug.

I will put in the box . . .

A year of summer holidays,
Beautiful orange fire melting,
A big block of ice burning.

My box is made from ice and fire,
With laughter on the lid,
Its hinges are the eyelids of a monkey.

I shall play in my box at the Bernabéu with those great players,
Messrs Fàbregas, Henry, Ronaldinho, Torres, Gerrard, Villa, Kaká
and C Ronaldo
And then land on a bright white cloud
Then finally sleep on it.

Owen Culliven (10)
Williamston Primary School, Murieston

My Magic Box

(Based on 'Magic Box' by Kit Wright)

I will put in my box . . .

Me running one mile and a half in thirteen minutes,
Me playing football with my tongue touching the gums.

I will put in my box . . .

Sledding down the hill at the bottom of my street,
Canoeing at the marsh at Midland in Canada,
Taking off on a plane and the whoosh when I am taking off.

I will put in my box . . .
My grandpa giving me a huge hug
And my grandma giving me a big, big, big hug.

I will put in my box . . .

A year full of summer
And me at the top of the CN Tower
With Christmas and birthdays every month.

My box is made from the blue sea and the Pacific Ocean.

I will revel in my box . . .

Lying in a canoe in the sea
Sleeping in that canoe and the relaxing sounds of the waves in the sea
And the canoe moving backwards and forwards, helping me
to fall asleep.

Grant Gourley (10)
Williamston Primary School, Murieston

My Magic Box

(Based on 'Magic Box' by Kit Wright)

I will put in my box . . .

The taste of fresh chocolate from Bourneville,
The smell of pizza from Pizza Hut,
The feeling of singing to myself.

I will put in my box . . .

Going sledding with my family,
Sitting on the balcony watching people go by,
Standing watching a dolphin show.

I will put in my box . . .

A big hug and kiss from my family,
My dad's best friend living in Scotland,
Seeing my granny again.

I will put in my box . . .

An ice skater on a sleigh
And a skier on the ice
And a pumpkin at Easter.

My box is made from gold, chocolate, silver, sweets
And a hint of coconut and nuts.

I shall ride in my box
Down the biggest mountain
And land on the nicest beach.

Emma Lynch (10)
Williamston Primary School, Murieston

My Magic Box

(Based on 'Magic Box' by Kit Wright)

I will put in the box . . .

The zoom of a super green field,
The brilliant play park of red and blue,
My friends playing a joke on one another.

I will put in the box . . .

The twang of a twilight bungee,
The splash of seals jumping,
The blue, yellow and red water park.

I will put in the box . . .

Laughter of my brother,
The smile of my mum,
Their business becoming a success.

I will put in the box . . .

A full year of Sundays,
A huge lake of chocolate,
Fireworks that can spell.

My box is made of dinosaur skin, green and red
With everlasting fun on the sides and chocolate in the corners
With hinges of a shark's eyelids.

I shall rock climb in my box higher than Mount Everest
Then float over a high tower, as red as fire.

Matthew Harrison (10)
Williamston Primary School, Murieston

My Magic Box

(Based on 'Magic Box' by Kit Wright)

I will put in my box . . .

Walking to the park on a summer's day,
The wind going through my hair when I am playing wall tig,
Walking around the street at night.

I will put in my box . . .

The loudest bang of a snowball hitting the ground,
The still blue pool at night, with lots of stars reflecting in the water,
The biggest dolphin from a dolphin show.

I will put in my box . . .

My parents' warm hugs,
My sister's weird laugh,
My sister on her first murder investigation.

I will put in my box . . .

Half a year of summer and the other half Christmas,
Singers skating all over the ice,
Skaters singing in a West End stage.

My box is made from chocolate and ice,
The lid is made from shooting stars with laughter in the corners,
The hinges are knee joints of horses.

I shall walk up Mount Everest with my box,
Then float into the night sky,
The colour of the sea.

Rebecca Broe (10)
Williamston Primary School, Murieston

My Magic Box

(Based on 'Magic Box' by Kit Wright)

I will put in my box . . .

The splash of swimming in beautiful deep water,
Going to my gran's house and having fun,
Me twiddling my hair around and around.

I will put in my box . . .

A stroll along the beach with,
Icy cold fingers during a snowball fight,
On holiday I like going to markets and shops.

I will put in my box . . .

A swish of my sister's beautiful smile,
My mum and my dad to cuddle me,
A wish for the future, a best friend who cares.

I will put in my box . . .

A never-ending summer with a sun so bright,
Flying monkeys so high,
Swinging birds from tree to tree.

My box is fashioned from a clear blue sky,
A lid of laughter and tears in the corner,
The hinges are the tears of a giraffe.

I shall dance in my box on the finest stage in the world,
I will float in the sky like an angel,
I will rest on the whitest cloud in the sky on a summer's day.

Sophie Jackson (10)
Williamston Primary School, Murieston

My Magic Box

(Based on 'Magic Box' by Kit Wright)

I will put in my box . . .

Wind blowing through my hair while I fly through the air on my bike,
One of the cleanest blades of grass from the pitch,
Playing the drums with one drummer out of Green Day.

I will put in my box . . .

A drip of the sea where I cut my shin,
The huge teeth of a great white shark,
Mopeds whizzing past my ears.

I will put in my box . . .

Terrible singing of my mum,
Seeing my brother play for RFC.

I will put in my box . . .

Dolphins on a boat, people in the water,
Summer all year long,
Adults doing the work, children teaching it.

My box is fashioned from . . .
Steel and rock from the sun,
Friends in the corners and crystal clear laughter,
The hinges are eagles wings.
I shall sit on my box while RFC lift it up,
While I fly away to the most beautiful island in the world.

Neil MacKinnon (10)
Williamston Primary School, Murieston

The Magic Box

(Based on 'Magic Box' by Kit Wright)

I will put in my box . . .

The shouting at Ibrox Stadium,
The lovely scent at Pizza Hut,
The sound of me singing to myself.

I will put in my box . . .

Building snowmen then jumping through them,
Jumping in a swimming pool, making a big splash,
Seeing a man on a dolphin next to a surfer.

I will put in my box . . .

All of my grandad's hugs,
And talking to my gran,
My wish is to see my grandad again.

I will put in my box . . .
Never-ending Christmas,
The Tooth Fairy fighting people,
Wrestlers taking people's teeth.

My box will be made from
Fire, ice and broccoli,
My lid is made from laughter and sadness in the corner,
The hinges will be the feet of a cheetah.

I will put in my box . . .

Playing football for Rangers
At Ibrox in Glasgow
With Barry Ferguson.

Corey Bryans (10)
Williamston Primary School, Murieston

My Magic Box

(Based on 'Magic Box' by Kit Wright)

I will put in my box . . .

Whizzing down the red ash path on my bike,
Going for fish and chips,
Talking to myself on a black night.

I will put in my box . . .

An igloo shaking,
A summer beach with people playing
And a bunch of dogs going wild.

I will put in my box . . .

The sound of my brother fighting,
Going on holiday with my grandma,
Watching my big brother swim for Scotland.

I will put in my box . . .

Never-ending birthdays,
Swimmers running
And runners swimming.

My box is made from . . .
Water, cake and dogs,
Laughter on the lid and lava in the corners
And dogs' tails for hinges.

I shall swim in my box
The English Channel
And land on a sandy beach on a black night.

Euan Dalgleish (10)
Williamston Primary School, Murieston

My Magic Box

(Based on 'Magic Box' by Kit Wright)

I will put in the box . . .

The lovely sound of my family and friends singing Happy Birthday to
me, with a lovely cake.

The smell of lasagne as I walk into a beautiful Italian restaurant,
The lovely feeling of me running my fingers through my hair.

I will put in the box . . .

The sound of me making snow angels as I lie in the beautiful
white snow,

The picture of me looking at the gleaming galaxies,
The gorgeous sound of dolphins swimming backwards and forwards.

I will put in the box . . .

The lovely bright colour of my nana's pink hair, as she runs her
fingers through her hair,

The sound of my kisses and hugs
And seeing my grandad for the first time.

I will put in the box . . .

The lovely picture of me picking my gran up,
My week of fantastic Thursdays,
The sound of fairies skating on shiny slippery ice,
The sound of a skater flying through the clouds.

My box is made from . . .
Silver with a sunset in Mexico
With love on the lid and hugs in the corner,
The hinges are made from swans' wings as they open.

I shall dance in my box,
I shall dance on stage at the West End
And then finally end up lying on a beautiful mountain.

Hayley Gillies (10)
Williamston Primary School, Murieston

My Magic Box

(Based on 'Magic Box' by Kit Wright)

I will put in my box . . .

The memory of going to festivals with my caring gran and grandad,
The memory of the band playing happily,
The feeling of my soft hair getting twirled.

I will put in my box . . .

Me at the side of the pool getting a fabulous tan,
Me and my family on a boat in France under the stars in the sky,
The most beautiful place was the little town of Couiller.

I will put in my box . . .

My brother's big strong bear hugs,
My mum's lovely soft hug,
I'd love to see my dad for more than a week.

I will put in my box . . .

A week full of Saturdays,
A dancer on skates,
And a figure-skater with tap shoes.

My box is made from . . .
The love my family gives to each other and rubies,
I will put humour on the lid and books in the corners,
My hinges are made from butterfly wings.

I shall play the piano at a musical concert in my box,
I shall get flung up in the air and land in soft freezing snow,
I shall land in a peaceful and quiet place with white horses, which
is a wonderful winter wonderland.

Jennifer McFadyen (10)
Williamston Primary School, Murieston

My Magic Box

(Based on 'Magic Box' by Kit Wright)

I will put in my box . . .

Walking in the woods with my dog,
Playing with my friends in my street,
Singing my heart out at choir.

I will put in my box . . .

A ski from Lapland,
Swimming with dolphins in Portugal,
Sunbathing in Spain beside the pool.

I will put in my box . . .

A hug from my great gran and great grandma,
A howl from my dog Kieko,
The warm feeling of when I hug my mum and dad.

I will put in my box . . .

A year full of summers,
Dolphins dancing on the beach,
Break dancers swimming about in the sea.

My box is made from . . .

Clear crystal, fine stones and diamonds,
Never-ending sweets,
My box has love on the lid and friendship in the corners.

I shall sing in my box . . .

All my favourite songs,
My voice singing on stage with Avril Lavigne and Robbie Williams.
I will sing in my box on stage for evermore.

Jennifer McLean (10)
Williamston Primary School, Murieston

My Magic Box

(Based on 'Magic Box' by Kit Wright)

I will put in my box . . .

The snap of the climbing tree branches,
The smooth pink silk in the clothes shop,
Two thin fingers braiding a strand of hair.

I will put in my box . . .

The swish of the ice skates rubbing on the ice,
The taste of saltwater on the Mediterranean Sea,
The Maori's of New Zealand performing their dance.

I will put in my box . . .

Baby Murray's cheery smile,
My granny Adam's gentle voice,
All my family from abroad, living in Scotland.

I will put in my box . . .

A year full of summers,
Spies shopping for designer clothes,
Ashley Lisdale hiding and sneaking.

My box is made from Tisdale
Silk and pink ribbon,
My lid is made from gleaming lilac diamonds,
My hinges are bluebird wings.

I shall flip over the Eiffel Tower and land on my feet in Paris.
Then I will lie myself down in the streets of Wellington amongst
the pinkest flowers.

Lucy Smith (10)
Williamston Primary School, Murieston

The Magic Box

(Based on 'Magic Box' by Kit Wright)

I will put in the box . . .

The wind rustling through the trees of Beecraigs,
The park's massive swings,
The feel of smooth hair.

I will put in my box . . .

Snowball fights in the whitest snow,
The salty smell beside the sea,
The fin of a basking shark.

I will put in my box . . .

My gran's hugs and kisses,
My sister's funny laugh
And the sight of my great grandpa.

I will put in my box . . .

A month full of birthdays,
Actors playing games of football,
Footballers playing parts in plays.

My box is made from . . .
The finest ice, snow and copper,
It has fun on the lid and love in the corners
And it's hinges are crocodile jaws.

I will swim with dolphins in my box,
Through the lovely blue sea
And land on a sandy beach in the deepest night.

Rachel Boden (10)
Williamston Primary School, Murieston

My Magic Box

(Based on 'Magic Box' by Kit Wright)

I will put in the box . . .

The splash of cool water,
Some fresh air
And the first word from a baby.

I will put in the box . . .

The break of a wave on the smooth surface of the sand,
Some crumbling sand in the sea,
Shells washing upon the surface.

I will put in the box . . .

The joyful laugh of my sister,
A strand of my mum's hair
And my dad's voice.

I will put in the box . . .

My dream to run free in a cool breeze,
A hand running through a cool lake
And a bright yellow sun.

My box is made from . . .

A silky breeze for the blue sky
And a melted flake of ice,
Plus a frozen snowdrop.

I shall swim in my box,
On the biggest waves ever,
With fish and dolphins around me.

Hannah Ritchie (10)
Williamston Primary School, Murieston

My Magic Box

(Based on 'Magic Box' by Kit Wright)

I will put in the box . . .

The sharp snap of the twig in the deep, dark woods,
The cha-ching of the cash register at the shops,
The suck of a little girl sucking the tip of her pinkie.

I will put in the box . . .

A dog rolling in the snow then shaking ferociously to get it off,
The splash of the kids jumping in and out of the clean blue pool,
The sound of kids screaming going down a steep roller coaster.

I will put in the box . . .

My nana stroking my hand while she talks to me in her quiet voice,
The crinkles beside my dad's eyes when he smiles at me,
To see my mum lie back and give a sigh of relief because
I have been good.

I will put in my box . . .

A decade full of Christmases
Martians on our planet
And humans on Mars.

My box is made from
Galaxy and puffy white clouds,
With ballet dancers on the lid and hugs and kisses in the corners,
Its hinges are the eyelids of a polar bear sleeping at the North Pole.

I will drum in my box
In front of the Queen and millions of other people,
After that I will bring my grandad back,
Then I will gently float up to the sky and land on a shiny white cloud.

Taylor Reid (9)
Williamston Primary School, Murieston

My Magic Box

(Based on 'Magic Box' by Kit Wright)

I will put in the box . . .

The beautiful music of the song me and my mum sing when we
go to Glasgow,
The long cycle path and my violet bike,
The warm feeling when I curl my hair.

I will put in the box . . .

The noise of when I am bashing my hands together when
I'm making snowballs,
The salty feeling when the sea washes up on my hands,
The click-clack, click-clack of high heels from a person wearing
a diamond sari.

I will put in my box . . .

The laughter of a baby child,
My grandad's hugs and kisses,
To see my uncle with a smile on his face with his new wife.

I will put in my box . . .

Half a year of winter and half a year of summer,
A warrior dancing on ice
And a figure skater fighting.

My box is fashioned from ice and diamonds,
With love on the lid and my grandad's tears in the corners.
My hinges are made from dove's wings.

I shall paint in my box with Charles Reine Makintosh,
The greatest waterfall ever created.
And end in the Heavens of my God, my family and my friends,
that's all.

Kiran Sandhu (9)
Williamston Primary School, Murieston

My Magic Box

(Based on 'Magic Box' by Kit Wright)

I will put in my box . . .

The snapping jaws of an angry crocodile,
A nine foot snake hunting its prey,
Someone walking along a beach with red stones.

I will put in the box . . .

A flying fox five miles off the ground,
A giant seesaw the colour of blood,
A tower ten miles off the ground, the colour of the sky.

I will put in the box . . .

A person surfing on 10 foot waves,
Two years full of snowy Christmases,
Two hot summers each year.

I will put in the box . . .

My lovely gran's laugh,
My cool grandpa's big hugs,
My mum's great smiles.

My box is made from gold, diamonds and steel,
There is happiness on the lid and speed in the corner,
The hinges are made from eagle wings.

I shall be a very successful sea fisherman in my box
And fish all over the world then wash ashore on a diamond beach.

Mark Beattie (10)
Williamston Primary School, Murieston

My Magic Box

(Based on 'Magic Box' by Kit Wright)

I will put in my box . . .

My colourful ribbons blowing in the wind,
Going to festivals and hearing the crowd cheer,
When I feel sad the cushion is my calling.

I will put in my box . . .

The swoosh of sledging,
The feeling of proudness when you reach the top of a mountain.
Me, in the seat of a roller coaster.

I will put in my box . . .

My dad lifting me upside down,
My uncle calling me 'princess',
Seeing my gran Chalmers again.

I will put in my box . . .

A generation of Christmases,
Miss Vincent in a golf suit,
Tiger Woods in Miss Vincent's clothes.

My box is made from
Glitter and icy stars, sweets for the top.
Happiness in the light and tragedy in the shadows.

I will experiment in my box,
I shall do the greatest experiment that will save human lives.

Hannah Adams (9)
Williamston Primary School, Murieston

My Magic Box

(Based on 'Magic Box' by Kit Wright)

I will put in my box . . .

A scream from the water slides at M and D's,
A trip as a family to Frankie and Benny's,
The way I twiddle my ears.

I will put in my box . . .

A slice of a blade touching the ice,
The eyes light up as they see the fireworks behind the castle.
The splash of Shamu leaping up from the water.

I will put in my box . . .

My mum's loud laugh,
My cousin holding my hand and laughing,
Seeing my dad have a better job.

I will put in my box . . .

A year full of Christmases,
Figure-skaters cooking in a kitchen,
Chefs skating on ice.

My box is made from
Chocolate and love hearts,
With shooting stars on the lid and laughter in the corner,
My hinges are made from crocodiles' mouths opening and closing.

I shall go around America in my box with my family and friends.
I will land in sunny Magic Kingdom in Florida outside the castle
with the bluest sky.

Rebecca Bain (10)
Williamston Primary School, Murieston

My Magic Box . . .

(Based on 'Magic Box' by Kit Wright)

I will put in the box . . .

A golden bike that goes zooming down the hill in style,
I like to go zooming on my bike for a cheese pizza,
I like to wiggle my ear all day on the sofa.

I will put in the box . . .

A silver sledge that goes zooming down the hill,
A quad bike that always wins on every race,
A speed boat speeding down the beautiful Nile.

I will put in the box . . .

My sister's most beautiful smile,
My uncle and me running down the golden beach,
My baby sister getting married in the church.

I will put in the box . . .

December every month in Scotland, beautiful white snow all year,
Ninja's quad biking around the course,
Quad bikers fighting furiously with each other.

My box is made from . . .
Fire which burns all around, with a Chinese dragon laughing to death,
Chocolate which tells secrets under real gold,
The brown eyes of my dog.

I will quad bike down the biggest hill in my box
And I will travel to the North Pole,
I will meet Santa and spend Christmas together.

Ryan Clarke (9)
Williamston Primary School, Murieston

My Magic Box

(Based on 'Magic Box' by Kit Wright)

I will put in my box . . .

The chatter of the actors when I go the cinema,
The scent of cheese pizza I get from Pizza Hut,
The way I bite my finger and get teeth marks.

I will put in my box . . .

The crunch I hear when a snowball hits a body,
The smell of restaurants as the Florida parade goes by,
The splash of Shamu diving underwater.

I will put in my box . . .

The laugh of my brother,
The first smile of my step-brother,
My mum getting a job closer to home.

I will put in my box . . .

Never-ending summer with a very yellow sun,
A spaceman winning a swimming race,
A swimmer travelling to space.

My box is made from . . .

Chocolate and gold stars that shimmer,
On the lid there is laughter and smiles in the corner,
The hinges are butterflies' wings fluttering.

I shall swim in the box for miles and miles across the Atlantic,
Then I will swim to a silver, cloudy, peaceful place.

Eilidh Jack (10)
Williamston Primary School, Murieston

My Magic Box

(Based on 'Magic Box' by Kit Wright)

I will put in my box . . .

The wind in my hair as I flip,
The breeze in my face as I run at the park,
Me swinging on my chair.

I will put in my box . . .

The coldness of a snowball fight,
Me playing at the pool with my friends,
The water hitting my face when dolphins jump out the pool.

I will put in my box . . .

My cousin laughing in my face,
My grandad's warm hug,
All my family, at Christmas dinner.

I will put in my box . . .

A never-ending Christmas,
A clown teaching,
Miss Vincent with a red nose.

My box is made from
Chocolate and sugar,
With laughter on the lid and love in the corners,
The wings of an eagle are the hinges.

I shall play football all around the world with Rangers
And float over the Atlantic on a pinkie cloud in my box.

Abbie Smith (10)
Williamston Primary School, Murieston

My Magic Box

(Based on 'Magic Box' by Kit Wright)

I will put in my box . . .

The sound of people cheering and chanting at football matches,
The sound of people's feet stomping on the ground when walking
around the shopping centre,
The sound of traffic beeping their horns in a traffic jam.

I will put in my box . . .

Burning rubber on the go-karts in Tenerife,
The whoosh of the cord bungee-jumping in Mallorca,
The handshake of Mickey Mouse at Universal Studios in Florida.

I will put in my box . . .

The sound of my gran's booming laugh,
A memory of all my family holidays,
A picture of all my family together.

I will put in my box . . .

The sound of monkeys flying through the air,
A picture of someone walking on lava without hurting themselves,
A picture of hovering people through the clouds.

My box is made from
Real icicles that never melt, hanging down from the lid,
A bit of lava to make the lid,
The outline is made from gold.

I will put in my box . . .

Me doing well, being a forensic scientist when I am older,
Swimming in the Olympics and winning the gold medal,
Becoming the best swimmer in Scotland.

Victoria Broe (10)
Williamston Primary School, Murieston

My Magic Box

(Based on 'Magic Box' by Kit Wright)

I will put in my box . . .

The sweetest laugh from a cheerful friend,
The bite from a delicious Domino's pizza,
The gentlest touch from two fingertips.

I will put in my box . . .

A crunch of a snowball crashing past my face,
The smell of the saltiest seas washing the seashells,
The sparkle from the smallest stars.

I will put in my box . . .

The chuckle from my grandad in his best clothes,
The first giggle from the sweetest cousin
And the biggest smile on my mum's face.

I will put in my box . . .

A year full of family Christmases,
The greatest dancers cooking in a steaming hot kitchen,
A fab cook doing a terrible dance on the biggest stage.

My box is made from . . .

Multicoloured candy and gorgeous ruby-red gems,
The lid is made from warm hugs and sloppy kisses and
hilarious jokes in the corner,
It's hinges are made from the wings of a colourful butterfly.

I will dance and act in my box, starring in all the fabulous shows
on the West End stage,
I will lay on a ruby pink cloud and float to the brightest stars.

Emily Jepson (10)
Williamston Primary School, Murieston

My Magic Box

(Based on 'Magic Box' by Kit Wright)

I will put into the box . . .

The roars of Tynecastle as the game kicks off,
The ball hitting the back of the net as we score,
Watching the team celebrate as we win.

I will put into the box . . .

The cha-ching of money as I go on holiday,
Smelling the food on plane rides,
The shhhhh of snow as my sledge hits it.

I will put into the book . . .

My grandad shouting, 'hugs',
My auntie Susan giving me tickets to football matches,
Seeing my grandad make people laugh.

I will put into the box . . .

Six years full of presents,
Playing football on a golf course,
Playing golf with a football.

My box is made from
Emeralds that look like scales,
With fun on the lid and hugs in the corner,
It's hinges are made from the fingers of babies.

I shall play football with the crowd of Hamden cheering me on,
To end up at the Hearts Stadium where my football dreams come true,
To float into the blue sky with my maroon scarf.

Kieran Smith (10)
Williamston Primary School, Murieston

The Magic Box

(Based on 'Magic Box' by Kit Wright)

I will put in the box . . .

A guinea pig with 20 legs,
The scales from a piranha,
The leg of a 20ft shrimp.

I will put in the box . . .

A lion's last roar,
A dinosaur's skull,
A 14st snail.

I will put in the box . . .

The treasure of a thousand worlds,
The solution to world hunger,
A sand monitor singing soundlessly through the sand.

I will put in the box . . .

60 cups of tea,
An avalanche from Mount Everest,
An axe from an executioner.

My box is made of . . .

Steel of a sunken bridge and wood,
The hinges are beaks of eagles,
It has skulls painted on the lid.

I will skydive in my box,
I will fly in my box,
I will surf in my box.

Nathan Broe (10)
Williamston Primary School, Murieston

The Magic Box

(Based on 'Magic Box' by Kit Wright)

I will put in the box . . .

Sunset on a summer night,
The smell of chocolate
And a top corner goal at the world finals.

I will put in the box . . .

Shiny new football trainers more comfy than a bed,
Shining stars shimmering on a summer night
And the first smile of a baby.

My box is fashioned from . . .
Gold, ice and steel welded together by dragon fire,
It's hinges are the claw joints of demon dragons.

I will ride in my box,
Across space five times the speed of light,
Then come across a new galaxy with a blue sun.

Zach Keane (10)
Williamston Primary School, Murieston

The Magic Box

(Based on 'Magic Box' by Kit Wright)

I will put into my box . . .

A blanket as soft as the snow,
A pretty dress made of soft velvet
And a playful puppy playing in the pretty evening.

I will put in the box . . .

The smell of a tasty cake made by fairies,
A dolphin gliding in the sea
And a soft twinkle of a twinkle star.

The box is made from
Gold and silver with stars on the roof and butterflies in the corners,
The lock is made of little animals that prance during and in the night.

I shall play in my box,
I will make art of the finest drawings
And tell all my worries to the box that I like.

Amy Denton (10)
Williamston Primary School, Murieston

I Will Put In The Box

(Based on 'Magic Box' by Kit Wright)

I will put in the box . . .

A black eye of an old man,
A poor man with the last one pound note,
A thousand eyes of the biggest of the biggest fish.

I will put in the box . . .

The boot of a big man bouncing on the black sand,
The fingertips of a fat man freezing a fresh fish,
A leaping leopard looking at a lighthouse.

I will put in the box . . .

The sour sweet of Sam's secret factory,
The zipping of a zooming car,
The dripping drip of plastic that doesn't make a sound.

I will put in the box . . .

A second moon on Earth,
The heat from the sun to go to Mars,
Neptune to have light.

The outside of my box is made from . . .

The graffiti of the best in the world,
The lid is made from solid gold.

I will draw on solid gold paper
And write with a platinum pencil.

Robbie Simpson (10)
Williamston Primary School, Murieston

I Will Put In The Box

(Based on 'Magic Box' by Kit Wright)

I will put in the box . . .

A white Christmas,
The purr of a newborn kitten,
The touch of a silky scarf.

I will put in the box . . .

The splash of a dolphin,
The sweet smell of sugar,
My little sister's laugh.

I will put in the box . . .

The smell of a violet lavender,
A very tall giraffe,
My favourite song and movie star.

I will put in the box . . .

A wish spoken with wisdom and wonder,
A Spanish song sung in English,
A ginormous book full of fairy tales.

My box is decorated all over with stars
And a gold keyhole ever so smooth,
My box is coloured in pink, white and blue.

I shall read every book and sing every song in my box,
I shall smell all the lavender flowers in my box,
I will wish for a white Christmas.

Sarah Wallace (10)
Williamston Primary School, Murieston

The Magic Box

(Based on 'Magic Box' by Kit Wright)

I will put in the box . . .

A soft silk blanket,
A hard part of wood with fun things on the top,
A rough tarantula with hairy legs,
Nothing will make me stop.

I will put in the box . . .

A tasty meal,
Spicy and hot,
Ready to eat,
It will be a spicy pizza pie with tomatoes on the top,
You will eat and eat,
Until the sun is down,
But the moon is up.

I will put in the box . . .

A smile of me,
A dress made of silk,
You and me playing all playfully and happy,
The daytime sun
And the night-time moon
And all the good times of me.

I will put in the box . . .

A shining moon,
An Indian girl in a pinkie silky sari,
The clothing of an old cowboy.
I see a dolphin,
It shall go in the box,
A special part of me too.

My box has stars all over the place
And it has five stripes in colours greeny grass,
Fire-type red,
Blue as the sea
And white snow
And me on the box wearing a silk sari.

I shall surf in the box
On a flying silk sari,
Me sitting on the moon,
Relaxing on the bed,
Waiting for more.

Sahdia Ahmed (9)
Williamston Primary School, Murieston

The Magic Box

(Based on 'Magic Box' by Kit Wright)

I will put in the box . . .

A white Christmas,
Motorbikes going *vroom, vroom,*
The glowing light of a star in the black sky.

I will put in the box . . .

A football in the back of the net,
The maddest scientist in the world,
The sun shining in the blue sky.

My box is made of glass and ice
And on the top it is painted blue with ice footballs,
The hinges are a dinosaur's finger joint.

In my box I will swim in the blue sea
And I will run across the beach.

Craig Wright (9)
Williamston Primary School, Murieston

The Magic Box

(Based on 'Magic Box' by Kit Wright)

I will put in the box . . .

The smell of coconut milk from America,
A mouse chasing a cat!
A baby riding on a dog!

I will put in the box . . .

A compass which tells you what you want,
A book sewn in silk that smells of a sweet summer scent,
A purple moon!

I will put in the box . . .

A library full of gold,
A cold fire,
An alien with glasses.

My box is made of . . .

Fine blue velvet,
With shiny diamonds to decorate
And the stand is made of wood but painted silver.

If I were in the box . . .

I would visit all the beaches,
Climb all the mountains
And listen to all the secrets.

Kiera Carmody (10)
Williamston Primary School, Murieston

The Magic Box

(Based on 'Magic Box' by Kit Wright)

I will put in my box . . .

The smell of melted chocolate,
The big invisible horse,
A magical leaf from the great tree.

I will put in my box . . .

The ugliest monster with a lolly,
A new universe with 18 planets,
A baby driving a spaceship.

I will put in my box . . .

A golden dragon,
The biggest spider you have ever seen,
A flying cat,
A big bang from the blue balloon.

My box looks like . . .

A shining star of silver,
It is made of platinum with gold and blue lining,
The hinges are of tiger's teeth.

I will sail around the world on my box,
I will dig to the centre of the Earth on my box.

Michael Laird (10)
Williamston Primary School, Murieston

The Magic Box

(Based on 'Magic Box' by Kit Wright)

I will put in the box . . .

The smell of chocolate melting in the microwave.
The taste of a prepared pepperoni pizza.
The touch of silk swaying on a spring day.

I will put in the box . . .

A gymnast on a beautiful bucking black horse
And a horse rider on a bendy beam.
A hairdresser happily cutting someone's hair.

My box is fashioned by . . .

Stars bright and colourful.
Ribbons that sparkle and shine
With blue ice-cold icicles.

What I'll do in the box
I shall do cartwheels and round-offs.
I will ice skate on an Olympic ice rink.
I shall ride on the back of the whitest polar bear.

Hayley Galloway (10)
Williamston Primary School, Murieston

The Magic Box

(Based on 'Magic Box' by Kit Wright)

I will put in the box . . .

The sand swishing on the seashore,
The roar of the waves,
The dogs barking in the morning.

I will put in the box . . .

The smell of petrol,
People delivering pizza,
A scuba-diver, eating a piece of cake.

I will put in the box . . .

A mint chocolate ice cream,
The icing on the top of a cake,
A bunch of apples on the treetop.

I will put in the box . . .

A baby brother laughing away,
A rabbit hopping all over the place,
A dog jumping to catch a fly.

Melissa Nisbet (9)
Williamston Primary School, Murieston

The Magic Box

(Based on 'Magic Box' by Kit Wright)

I will put in my box . . .

A man playing football in the deep blue sea,
A diver trying to play football on the green grass football pitch,
A million stars above my house at night.

I will put in my box . . .

Diving boards that go into the deep blue waters,
The sweet smell of petrol when you go to the petrol station.

I will put in my box . . .

A burger with tomato sauce, just the right amount,
A snow snake slithering through the snow,
The Disney Castle lit up at night with the river around it.

My box is made of . . .

Gold and diamonds with stars and wishes on top
And yellow, blue, red and silver around the edges,
If you open the box, it will explode with dreams, hopes and wishes.

Katy Lee (10)
Williamston Primary School, Murieston

The Magic Box

(Based on 'Magic Box' by Kit Wright)

I will put in the box . . .

A blazing blue sun,
The swish of the sea swerving backwards
And a monkey that does not like bananas.

I will put in the box . . .

A cowboy on a dinosaur,
A 100-year-old grandmother
And a teardrop of a giant.

My box is fashioned of gold and steel.
It has stars on the lid and spikes in the corners
And it has lots and lots of silver locks.

I shall ski down a big white mountain,
Fall down the big mountain
And spit out of the box.

Connor McNaughton (10)
Williamston Primary School, Murieston

The Magic Box

(Based on 'Magic Box' by Kit Wright)

I will put in the box . . .

Kindness and care in every way,
A delicious pear, fresh from the vine
And the first drop of a winter snow.

I will put in the box . . .

A puppy flying through the night sky,
A mouse being shot out of a cannon
And the blast of blossoms still in bloom.

I will put in the box . . .

A mouse chasing an owl,
The horn of a horse on Hogmanay
And no more definitions in a dictionary!

I will put in the box . . .

A cheetah, the speed of a snail,
Dull grey turning to glimmering silver
And a baby climbing onto the biggest jeep.

My box is designed with colours galore,
Stars, art and writing all over.
A face of happiness on each hinge,
Also, the smallest spots of gold.

My box will uncover everyone's dreams,
Their wishes, their wants, their needs
And everything more.
This is what my box will do, yes it is true . . .

Nathan Campbell (10)
Williamston Primary School, Murieston

The Magic Box

(Based on 'Magic Box' by Kit Wright)

I will put in the box . . .

Some freshly mown grass so green and bright
The smell of a barbecue on a summer's night
And the scent of summer flowers.

I will put in the box . . .

A yummy pizza with double cheese
A cake with sweets on top
And the best fruit salad.

I will put in the box . . .

The sound of delighted dogs barking
The laughter of children playing
And the sound of bubble paper popping.

I will put in the box . . .

A lazy leopard with stripes
A lion with blue toes
And a terrible tiger with spots.

My box will be made
From jewels of gold and ice
The hinges from 15th Century goblins.

I will skydive in my box
Off a high cliff into the sea.

Niamh Armstrong (10)
Williamston Primary School, Murieston

The Magic Box

(Based on 'Magic Box' by Kit Wright)

I will put in my box . . .

A burning barbecue
And some flowers on a summer night
With a big blue sea.

I will put in my box . . .

My favourite animals
Poodles and border collies.
Dolphins diving in and out of the sea
And a silver, slimy, slithering snake.

I will put in my box . . .

My favourite noises,
A dog barking with the sea in the background,
I love stamping on bubble paper when I get gifts.

My box will be a magic box because it will have
My favourite things in it.

I will smell and look for my favourite things,
My box will be my favourite.

Jade Spence (10)
Williamston Primary School, Murieston

The Magic Box

(Based on 'Magic Box' by Kit Wright)

I will put in the box . . .

A boy with a rattle,
A baby with a petrol can,
The smell of curry sauce.

I will put in the box . . .

A monkey driving a mini motor,
A snail running from a cat,
A shiny star.

I will put in the box . . .

A cat with a shotgun,
A dog with a bone,
A melon on a horse.

This is what my box is made of . . .

Silver magic bits of wood,
With a gold lock,
With a shining yellow colour.

Jack Meldrum (10)
Williamston Primary School, Murieston

The Magic Box

(Based on 'Magic Box' by Kit Wright)

I will put in the box . . .

A dolphin skydiving,
A whizzing wizard's spell gone wrong,
And an elephant chasing a mouse.

I will put in the box . . .

A thirteenth month,
A jumping snail
And a slow hare.

I will put in the box . . .

A whining worm who is warm,
A baby driving a car
And a dad in a cot.

I will put in the box . . .

The death of an evergreen plant,
A bird scuba-diving,
And a horn that can't hoot.

My box is full of colours so bright,
Its hinges are made of raven claws covered in ice,
And it is made of inedible chocolate.

I will fly in my box,
I will watch the sun set and rise,
I will play in my box until my heart stops beating.

Blair Gibson (9)
Williamston Primary School, Murieston

The Magic Box

(Based on 'Magic Box' by Kit Wright)

I will put in the my box . . .

A shimmering star that shoots about in the night sky,
A sniff of a jasmine flower,
A strong current from the Atlantic Ocean.

I will put in my box . . .

A tiny lion cub with an extremely loud roar,
A golden snitch that glimmers in the light,
A soft burger.

My box is made from dark blue glass,
Its hinges are made from dead stars that still glow,
On the lid there is multicoloured glitter.

In my box I shall glide and wash ashore
On the golden islands of Saturn.

Aisha Lawlor (9)
Williamston Primary School, Murieston

My Magic Box

(Based on 'Magic Box' by Kit Wright)

I will put in the box . . .

My dad's house,
Cycling.

I will put in the box . . .

A sledge to go on,
Me swimming with my dad in a big pool.

I will put in the box . . .

My family,
My brother laughing and playing
Money from my grandad.

Nathan Magee (10)
Williamston Primary School, Murieston

The Magic Box

(Based on 'Magic Box' by Kit Wright)

I will put in the box . . .

The silkiest rug with a shimmering light,
The sparkle of a star on a summer night,
6 sweet cakes made from fairy dust.

I will put in the box . . .

The light of the sun and moon,
The smallest secrets
And the swish of the bluest ocean.

My box is made of . . .

Silver, shining stars,
The hinges are full of secrets
And the corners are made from sharp painted silver.

I will rock climb in my box
And land in victory.

Natasha Duffin (9)
Williamston Primary School, Murieston

The Magic Box

(Based on 'Magic Box' by Kit Wright)

I will put in the box . . .

A snapping, swerving snake,
A sweet taste of sugar,
A magnificent jumping dolphin.

I will put in the box . . .

The smile of brothers
I like the smell of melted chocolate,
I like to see people jumping into pools.

The hinges are made of bronze
There are stars, yellow and black
One side is yellow and black.

I shall jump into the box
And do the biggest Mexican wave
And do stunts in the street
I will fly to different places.

Joe Mitchell (10)
Williamston Primary School, Murieston

Rugby

R ugby is just right for me
U nstoppable tries and kicks
G o on, try and stop me lad, no chance mate
B one-breaking tackles
Y ou should try it!

Stefan Cameron (11)
Yetholm Primary School, Yetholm

My Best Friend

My best friend is pretty,
My best friend is funny,
My best friend is caring and loving,
My best friend likes toast and honey.

My best friend is barking mad,
My best friend is wriggly,
My best friend is eager to see you,
My best friend is sniffy.

My best friend is bonkers,
My best friend is silly too,
My best friend is clumsy,
I bet you can't guess who!

My best friend is daft,
My best friend is waggy,
My best friend has a wet nose,
My best friend is our dog *Maggie!*

Molly Ingledew (11)
Yetholm Primary School, Yetholm

Trampoline

Up down, up down, I'm bouncing really high
Up down, up down, see me I can fly
Down up, down up, puddle in the middle
Down up, down, down, oh no I'm sitting in it.
I am a superhero, flying in the sky
Got to mind my head up here
You'll never guess why
The Statue of Liberty is very, very near
If I bounce hard enough,
I could poke her in the ear.
Up down, up down, I'm bouncing really high
Up down, up down, see me I can fly.

Sophie Ingledew (7)
Yetholm Primary School, Yetholm

If I Cross

If I cross the river,
If I cross the sea,
Will I ever see you again,
Or will it just be me?

If I open my eyes,
If I open my heart tonight,
Will I ever see you again,
Or will it just be me?

If I cross the quicksand,
If I cross the desert,
Will I ever see you again,
Or will it just be me?

If I open my eyes,
If I open my heart tonight,
Will I ever see you again,
or will it just be me?

If I cross the ice,
If I cross the snow,
Will I ever see you again,
Or will it just be me?

If I open my eyes,
If I open my heart tonight,
Will I ever see you again,
Or will it just be me?

If I cross the mud,
If I cross the meadow,
Will I ever see you again,
Or will it just be me?

Rachel Louise Dickson (11)
Yetholm Primary School, Yetholm

Young Writers Information

We hope you have enjoyed reading this book - and that you will continue to enjoy it in the coming years.

If you like reading and writing poetry drop us a line, or give us a call, and we'll send you a free information pack.

Alternatively if you would like to order further copies of this book or any of our other titles, then please give us a call or log onto our website at www.youngwriters.co.uk

Young Writers Information
Remus House
Coltsfoot Drive
Peterborough
PE2 9JX

(01733) 890066